WHALES

WHALES

Kara Zahn

GALLERY BOOKS
An Imprint of W.H. Smith Publishers, Inc.
New York, New York 10016

A FRIEDMAN GROUP BOOK

Published by GALLERY BOOKS
An imprint of W.H. Smith Publishers, Inc.
112 Madison Avenue
New York, New York 10016

ISBN 0–8317–9412–7

WHALES
was prepared and produced by
Michael Friedman Publishing Group, Inc.
15 West 26th Street
New York, New York 10010

Art Director/Designer: Mary Moriarty
Photo Editor: Christopher Bain
Production Manager: Karen L. Greenberg

Typeset by Mar + x Myles Graphics, Inc.
Color separations by South Sea International Press Ltd.
Printed and bound in Hong Kong by Leefung-Asco Printers, Ltd.

The illustration on page 32 by Pieter Folkens
appeared first in **The Sea World Book of Whales**,
courtesy of Harcoúrt, Brace, Jovanovich.

64771

Dedication

In memory of my grandfather, who worked in the Brooklyn Navy yard, and my beloved grandmother who somehow put up with him. Know that your zest for life and love of the sea is still inspiring.

Acknowledgments

Thanks to Dr. Larry Barnes, Curator of Vertebrate Paleontology at the Los Angeles County Museum of Natural History, and Joan Ward, Public Information Officer at the University of California at Santa Cruz for graciously extending their valuable time and expertise. For the generous contribution of their original artwork, thanks are also due to Jenny Wardrip and Annette Whelan. And a very special thanks to Pieter Folkens for his wisdom and patience.

Contents

© Jeff Foott

Contents

They say the sea is cold, but the sea contains
The hottest blood of all, and the wildest, the most urgent.

All the whales in the wider deeps, hot are they, as they urge
on and on, and dive beneath the icebergs.
The right whales, the sperm whales, the hammer heads, the killers
there they blow, there they blow, hot wild white breath out of the sea

And they rock, and they rock, through the sensual ages
on the depths of the seven seas,
and through the salt they reel with drunk delight
and in the tropics tremble they with love
and roll with massive, strong desire, like gods.

—From "Whales Weep Not, " by D. H. Lawrence

Mankind's Eternal Muse

The biblical story of Jonah documents humans' fascination with whales. This fresco by Michelangelo appears on the Sistine Chapel in Rome.

The fish that isn't a fish, the mammal that seems to bear no likeness to man, the whale has sustained our fascination since the beginning of mankind. At once an icon and a metaphor, the sea's most mighty monarch permeates our history and culture—from tall tales to epic novels, canvas to celluloid, sea chantey to contemporary pop music. Although the earliest artistic renderings of the whale appear in crude Norwegian cave drawings dating back to approximately 5,000 B.C., the Greeks, who revered some whales and dolphins, were the first to depict their image with the accuracy of first-hand knowledge in drawings, poetry, fables, and song. In the fourth century B.C., Aristotle established himself as an early biologist with a book he called *History of Animals.* His entries on sea life were most prophetic, including concise behavioral examples of the order of the cetacea, or fish-like mammals, that includes whales, dolphins, and porpoises. Most of these observations were probably based on the dolphins inhabiting the waters around Aristotle's home on Lesbos, a Greek island off the coast of Turkey.

The whale also puts in one of its earliest written appearances in the pages of Genesis: "In the beginning . . . the earth was void and empty . . . the spirit of God moved over the waters . . . and God created the great whales, and every living and moving creature, which the waters brought forth, according to their kinds . . . And he blessed them, saying: Increase and multiply, and fill the waters of the sea." Even then, the whale had a foreboding personality as the symbolic protagonist in what is most likely the world's oldest fish story, that of a minor prophet, Jonah. Written anonymously in the fourth century B.C., "The Story of Jonah" counseled on the dangers of a narrowed sense of nationalism. According to the story, Jonah was commissioned by God to preach to the people of Nineveh, capital of the Assyrian empire, that they and all around them would be destroyed if they did not repent their wicked ways. However, because the Assyrians were the children of Israel's cruelest oppressors, Jonah boarded a sea-faring ship and fled rather than incur their wrath. When the boat was suddenly besieged by raging storms, the sailors prayed to God and asked Him what they had done to deserve His fury. Learning of Jonah's betrayal, they cast him overboard to save themselves. A stricken Jonah was then swallowed by a "great fish," presumably a whale, and imprisoned in the creature's belly for three days and nights. The whale, a vessel of the Lord's discontent, vomited him upon the Assyrian shores

F. Gironda. F.Bellu... F. Magnu...

4.

© Theodore DeBry, circa 1590

Early explorers to the New World documented the presence of whales in their maps. This one, drawn by the artist Jacques le Moyne de Morgues, who accompanied a French expedition to Florida in 1564, depicts the whale as a monstrous creature of the sea. This whale appears ready to attack the ship.

once he had agreed to resume his mission. Historians and philosophers believe the whale was in fact a religious rebuke for the Jews who at the time were retreating into communal exclusivity.

Religious politics aside, the horrific imagery of a man swallowed whole by a creature so enormous continued to be an artistic topic. The story repeatedly appeared in the monastic paintings and Islamic manuscript illustrations of the early Middle Ages, although these were naive and unrealistic renderings.

By the seventeenth century, however, the whale was no longer relegated to the realm of myth and symbolism. This new world of exploration and invention had built-in opportunities for derring-do. Elevated by his sense of accomplishment, mankind replaced his idols with heroic self-portraits. And nothing, outside of a battle, glorified man's courage or celebrated his supremacy quite like a painting of the whale industry.

The painters of the seventeeth century were keenly aware of their place as

F. Guate

F. Nastania

F. Flor

F.

Mexicani Sinus pars

The proportion of the ship to the whale in this le Moyne illustration reflects sailors' fear of what were then mysterious sea beasts. The creature's dual blowholes indicate that le Moyne based this drawing on a member of the mysticeti suborder.

keepers of historical record, and thus had a passion for accuracy. Among them was Adriaan van Salm (c. 1663 to 1720), who fashioned his pictures of naval vessels, battles, and whalers through a technique known as grisaille, elaborate sketches detailed in pen and India ink, or sepia, on a prepared white background. Van Salm's "A Whaling Scene" is a classic example of the clean lines and dimensional perspective made possible by this monochrome painting and drawing technique.

By 1769, whaling was an accepted theme, frequently found in the works of anonymous artists. Marine painting bloomed fully, however, in the late eighteenth century, in the newly burgeoning whalers' port of Kingston-upon-Hull, where a group of house and ship painters depicted their sudden booming industrialization and the strange beauty of the creatures who had made it possible. John Ward, an apprentice ship painter, was the principal artist among the Hull school's sea-inspired craftsmen. His initial visit to the whaling grounds produced his most vivid composition, "Hull Whalers in the Arctic." It is a work of striking detail that presents a first-hand account of a landscape plundered by man. In this powerful painting, a walrus, polar bear, sea turtle, and a flock of gulls all witness a cornered whale's brutal demise.

Similarly, William Bradford's marine realist paintings would incorporate the accuracy of the grisailles with the heightened sense of dramatic perspective introduced at the Hull school. "The Whaleship Northern Night," a typical vessel portrait, flaunts a new-found lyricism under Bradford's guidance. Despite the flat, draftsman-like quality of the ship itself, the water has a luminous sparkle and grace; the clouds are airy and bright, while the ship's sails appear to be softly billowing. There is even a trace of romanticized theatrics in his "Whaling in Northern Waters," a far bleaker look at a scene reminiscent of Ward's "Hull Whalers in the Arctic." Bradford's painting of a killing is harsher still because of its stark, lifeless foreground and rough-hewn landscape. The victorious whalemen, contrary to their great conquest, are but insignificant specimens against the horizon.

Albert Pinkham Ryder, another major marine painter of the late 1800s, painted with romantic passion in his depictions from literature about the sea. His representation of Jonah's plight carried far more emotional appeal than the early monastic drawings of Jonah done in the Middle Ages. A contemporary of Herman Melville (equally enraptured with the whale's sym-

North Wind Picture Archives

The rugged and dangerous whaling practices of yesteryear have fascinated artists for generations. This drawing of Native North Americans supposes their primitive methods for killing whales (inset). Whaling in nineteenth-century North America, as drawn by Oswald W. Drierly in "South Sea Whaling" (left), romantically depicts the rough seas and violence involved with whaling.

Perhaps the best known tale of a human encounter with a whale, the original *Moby-Dick* was published in 1851. This epic novel, an allegory of spiritual turmoil, is based on sailors' tales of sea monsters and on Herman Melville's ten years on the whaling ship *Acushnet*.

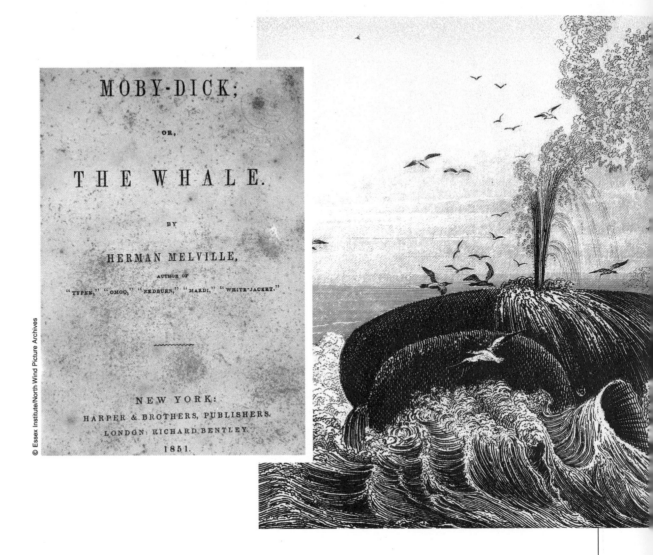

bolic possibilities), Ryder filled his canvas with the writhing chaos of churning waves and the darkly menacing whale in all its watery fury. Jonah is all but lost in the froth as the vision of God peers down from the heavens. It is a masterful interpretation of spiritual turmoil.

The whale in literature, as in art, emerged as a powerful symbol of man's need to embrace and harmonize with nature.

In the nineteenth century, when Albert Ryder was painting the cold and beastly whale that characterized Jonah's fall from grace, Herman Melville was plotting the course of *Moby-Dick*. In the January chill of 1841, Melville set sail from New Bedford as a crew member of the whaler *Acushnet*. At the start, he envisioned *Moby-Dick* as a factual narrative, but his subsequently colorful experiences on many whaling ships and far-off islands broadened his perspective. He acquired an insatiable lust for fine literature, indulging his fancy for Shakespeare, Hawthorne, and Elizabethan dramatists, as well as seventeenth-century essayists. As his artistic soul evolved, so did his

North Wind Picture Archives

Whalers lowered small wooden boats from the sides of their tall sailing ships to pursue and harpoon whales. While these row boats were easily maneuvered, structurally they were no match for the thrashing beast.

manuscript, his facts becoming symbols, his journal a treatise of myths and legends. Ten years after boarding the *Acushnet,* Melville's classic struggle of man and whale was published. Even today, there is debate about what "eternal truths" Melville discovered on that whaling ship. Psychologists maintain that the whaling crew is the incarnation of repressed sexuality; the great whale then becomes the ultimate phallus swimming in a watery womb of earthly temptations (an image later alluded to in D. H. Lawrence's "Whales Weep Not"). Religious moralists insist that Captain Ahab's stubborn pursuit of Moby-Dick represents man's willful disregard of God's natural providence, a theory in which the white whale personifies the amoral brute energies of a divine universe. Finally, sociologists view the story as an allegorical commentary on the socio/political development of American society at mid-century, the whalers revolting against the structure of an evil world with all of its injustice and despair festering in the monstrous body of the great whale. While the conclusions vary, one element remains constant;

© Jeff Foott

© Jeff Foott

Colorful and mythical in proportion, the whale is often portrayed in Pacific Northwest native art. This wood sculpture (above) is a tribute to the male killer whale. Note its soaring tail fin and the athletic thrust of its body as it's captured in mid-leap.

Totem poles pay homage to pagan gods and the unexplained forces of nature. This one on Vancouver Island in British Columbia, Canada (left) depicts one such god cradling the lifeless form of a great whale.

in each interpretation the whale symbolizes all that is wicked, treacherous, and deceitful in its time. This reputation is not easily lived down.

In 1953, movie producer Irwin Allen presented an undersea documentary based on the observations of renowned author/naturalist Rachel Carson, whose book, *The Sea Around Us,* had been a national best seller. His film of the same title won an Academy Award. Once again, the whale had an audience but, alas, as before, he was hopelessly typecast as one of the "great monsters of the deep." Allen's film reminisced on the past one hundred years, when whaling "enjoyed its golden age," and bemoaned with envy and a touch of remorse that whaling, although still highly profitable ("the take" being ninety million gallons [340 million liters] of oil per year) was now the chief domain of foreigners. A final, most incongruous image appeared on the screen: a lone whale, harpooned by a crew of husky sailors, lay dying, bleeding the sea red, while the voiceover prattled on that these "monsters" were "extremely difficult to kill."

The whale's reputation would be avenged in the 1970s; the environmental alarm had been sounded and man was experiencing his first tentative contacts with whales in captivity, which encouraged him to examine more closely his responsibilities regarding this great creature. A 50-foot (15-meter) sculpture of a fin whale, designed by Larry Foster, was raised in San Francisco Park to celebrate the sympathetic bond between man and marine mammal. To many, it looked like "The Time of the Whale" had indeed arrived. Perhaps for the first time since his death was lauded in sea chanteys, the whale would surface in pure song as the decade brought a brief flirtation with environmental "music": recordings of a thunderstorm, a waterfall, the sea's crashing waves, and the purely vocalized cries of the whale. The whale's indignant bellow was part of popular meditative/relaxation programs of the time. In 1970, zoologists Roger Payne and Frank Watlington recorded "Songs of the Humpback Whale" on Capitol Records, which sold more than one hundred thousand copies and was followed by "Deep Voices." The whale's stylized erotic syncopation inspired electronic music, and its influence may still be heard in some synthesized New Age music.

In 1975, folk-rock musicians David Crosby and Graham Nash sang a bittersweet tribute, "To the Last Whale." The first movement, entitled "A Critical Mass," was a haunting requiem, a latterday Gregorian chant, which expressed the mood eloquently. The rejoinder, "Wind on the Water," gave an unvarnished account of the whale's senseless slaughter: "It's not that we don't know... it's just that we don't want to care."

Another musical artist, Raffi, a popular children's folk singer, found positive inspiration in the grace of small white whales, the belugas, called sea canaries by early British sailors because of their lilting bird-like chatter. Seeing one at the Vancouver Aquarium reminded the singer/songwriter of children at play. His song, "Baby Beluga," was a pre-school hit and may likely become a traditional folk standard for children.

"If you sing a song about the beauty of a creature," Raffi said, "and people pick up on your feelings and appreciate this creature, perhaps they'll want to help protect it, to save it."

The theme of marine life continued to prosper in the 70s with the union of beauty and accuracy best defined by science illustrators, chief among them Pieter Arend Folkens. In 1979, a whale drawing he had done was selected as the logo of the Guild of National Science Illustrators. Shortly thereafter, he drew a pair of bottlenose dolphins, smiling serenely as they swam in unison against a dark background with a drape of sun-splashed bubbles. The poster, "Double Dolphins I," was acquired by the environmental protection group, Greenpeace. But the sweetly benevolent creatures struck such a responsive chord with the public that they soon became a merchandising phenomenon, and, along with marine mammal drawings of a similar theme, launched Folkens' whales and dolphins on to best-selling t-shirts, notebook covers, and beach towels. Today, Folkens' whale originals are worth many thousands of dollars.

A far cry from the 1950s, recent film has shown some of the most encouraging signs of improving man's understanding of the whale. No more the vicious killer of "Orca" movies, today the whale may be billed as the hero as in the phenomenally successful 1987 science fiction movie, *Star Trek IV: The Voyage Home,* in which the songs of two humpback whales (their special effects' miniatures sculpted by Pieter Folkens) save mankind. As the character Spock paraphrased the philosophy of Jacques Cousteau: "There are other forms of intelligence on earth... only human arrogance would assume the message must be for man."

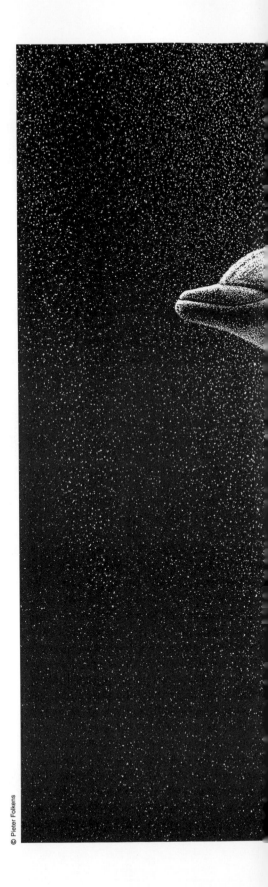

Premier illustrator of the cetacea, Pieter Arend Folkens launched his career with this picture that was done for Greenpeace.

CHAPTER TWO

The Creation of the Cetacea

The whale's physical likeness to the fish around him is really a concession to his environment. Whales are members of the order of Cetacea who possess many common attributes with man. They are warm-blooded, air-dependent creatures with elaborate brain structures. All things considered, how did they evolve so differently? Cetacean fossils date back more than 50 million years ago to the second-stage radiation of mammals. After four billion years of early evolution, sea creatures began to develop the first benchmark characteristics of higher life including fully functional jaws, a vertebral column, and a complete nervous system, beginning first with cold-blooded shark-like creatures. Centuries passed, and these creatures came out of their ocean habitats to populate the land. Their fins adapted into legs—this was the age of the reptiles. One hundred million years later, creatures with a high central temperature developed, marking them as warm-blooded. They were powerful, with quick energy and remarkable endurance.

In particular, one creature evolved into the first mammal-like reptile over 90 million years ago. Although there is still some debate, it seems likely that the first mammal was a diminutive insect-eater similar to a squirrel-like specimen called a "tupai," commonly called a tree shrew, an insect-eating primate found in the jungles of South East Asia. Oddly enough, this tiny creature shows evidence of being related to a disparate variety of mammal species, including the earliest mammals who lived when dinosaurs ruled the earth more than sixty-five million years ago. Like most mammals the tree shrew is quick and agile, generating its own body heat to provide fast energy. Scientists believe it holds the basic biological pattern for a multitude of species, some so disparate it challenges the imagination, including ant-eaters, desmans, moles, bats, and monkeys along with whales, dolphins, and porpoises.

Certain fossil remains have also lead paleontologists to believe that a wolf-like beast slowly took on the characteristics of aquatic adaptations of the whale. Its snout gradually elongated, inching up to its forehead, its nostrils and its legs shortened until the hind limbs completely disappeared. Within the modern whale, there are vestigial hipbones that once supported legs uselessly suspended in its hind quarters. The bones of their flippers resemble the bone structure of human hands, with five hidden extensions much like fingers. While the cetacean body has no neck, whale spines have the same cervical vertebrae found in terrestrial mammals. As an embryo, the whale fetus displays other unnecessary characteristics. It begins with four limbs, external genitals, and nostrils at the end of their snout. A rapid "evolution" of sorts is demonstrated within the womb: the front limbs become flippers; the hind legs disappeared and its tail developed a muscle that became the fluke; the "nostrils" settle in where a blowhole will be; and the genitals develop enclosed within a ventral slit. With its streamlined body and paddle-like appendages, the whale is now suited to swimming.

The first animals to take on these characteristics were the archaeocetes, or ancient whales. The link between the archaeocetes and the modern whale is believed to be *pakicetus*. In 1980, French and American scientists discovered the pakicetus skull at the base of the Himalayas in Pakistan. Scientists believe pakicetus is the best example of an animal adaptation between land and sea, the direct ancestor to the fully aquatic archaeo-

A proposed family tree of the modern whale forks into two main branches, the baleen and toothed whales.

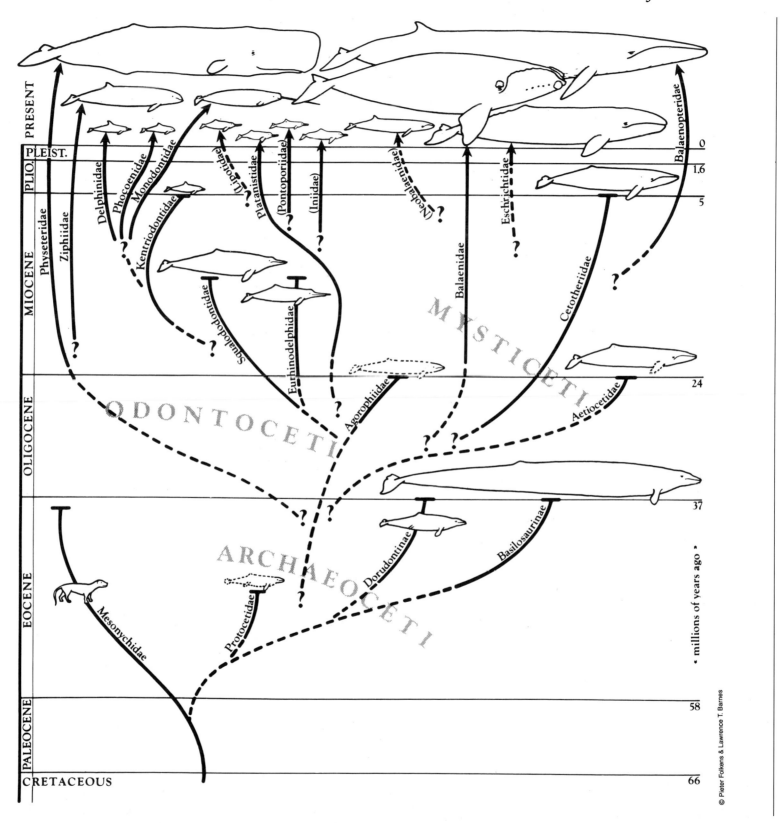

cetes. The archaeocetes flourished for fifteen million years before they became extinct. Five million years later, representatives of the modern cetacean suborders (mysticeti and odontoceti) were firmly established.

Most of the distinguishing traits we see today are the result of adaptations to environmental conditions and to exploit a given resource. The whale's great bulk, the result of layered blubber, helps him maintain his body temperature—a primary concern since water draws off heat twenty times faster than air. The furry hide that serves to insulate the land mammal helps to sustain its warmth by trapping air between the hair follicles. So, of course, the modern whale has discarded this, too, leaving only a few bristly hairs on the snout and, occasionally, the forehead and lower jaw.

The environment necessitated these changes and they were the cetcean's saving grace. By returning to the ocean, the whales averted a major evolutionary obstacle that had brought the downfall of their ancient predecessors. Like the whale, the dinosaur's ability to adapt its size to maintain body temperature regardless of the earth's climate worked to its advantage. But the dinosaur's ability to bulk up was limited by his bone structure. Because of this structural deficiency, a dinosaur's limbs would snap beneath the strain of too much weight, which he would have to gain to adjust to drastic drops in the surface temperature. The whale's skeletal system on the other hand developed primarily to insure speed and motion. Their massive bodies are supported by the gravitational pull of the ocean, allowing them to safely maintain whatever weight is necessary to comfortably endure their envirnoment.

The marine mammal retains a dependency on air that would seem to be a major drawback. However, whales breathe more efficiently than terrestrial mammals. With a normal breath, man clears approximately 15 percent of accumulated air from his lungs. In sharp contrast, the whale in one exuberant burst rids himself of 90 percent of his spent air. As a result, it breathes at extended intervals. In addition, the whale has developed a high concentration of myoglobin, a substance found in the muscle tissue that enables him to actually store oxygen.

An iron-based protein, the properties of myoglobin are very similar to that of the hemoglobin found in human muscle tissue. In most vertebrates, hemoglobin is a respiratory pigment found within the blood cells that brings oxygen to the body tissues or carries carbon dioxide away from them. Likewise the whale's myoglobin allows the whale to stay under water for extended periods of time at great depths because of its ability to maintain oxygen levels in the whale's tissue.

This fossilized skull of a fifteen-foot (four-meter) baleen whale (above) is smaller than any adult baleen living today. Discovered on Año Nuevo Island by a team from the University of California at Santa Cruz, the fossil is between twelve and fourteen million years old.

Right, top to bottom: Whales are believed to have evolved from land mammals such as this four-footed, wolf-like beast called mesonychid condylarth, a presumed evolutionary stage, to half-land, half-aquatic animals known as protocetus, to the archaeocetes, one of the last evolutionary stages before the modern whale. Note the evolution of the feet into flippers possessing fingerlike appendages on the protocetus to the smooth flippers of the archaeocete.

10 centimeters

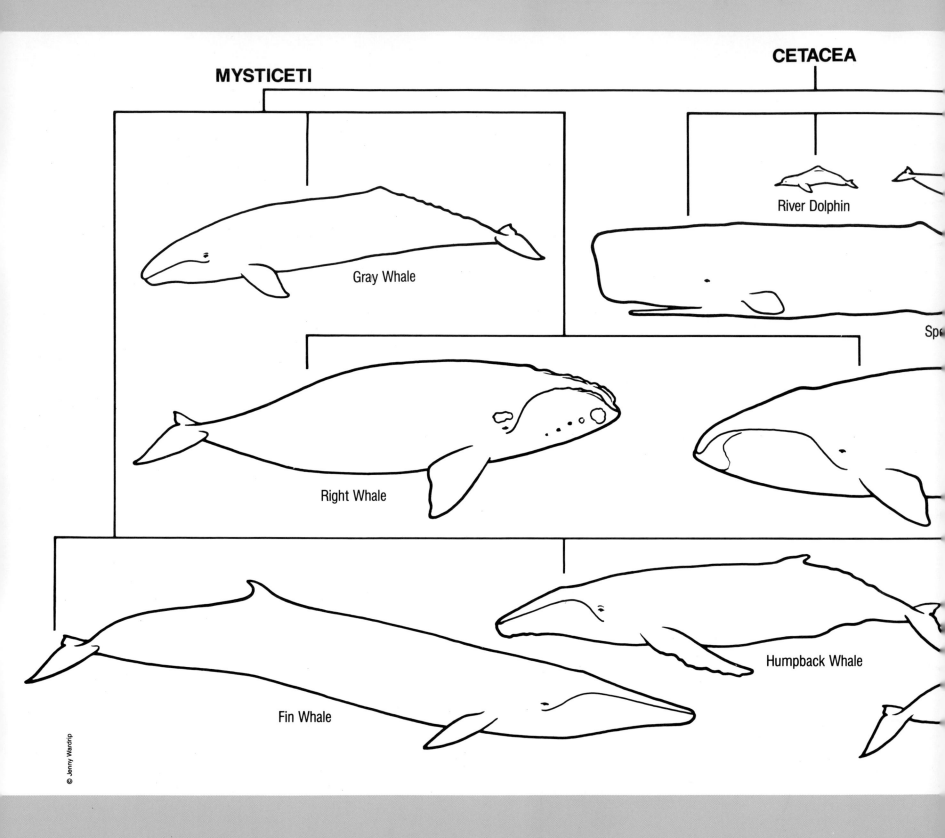

CETACEA

MYSTICETI

Gray Whale

River Dolphin

Sp...

Right Whale

Fin Whale

Humpback Whale

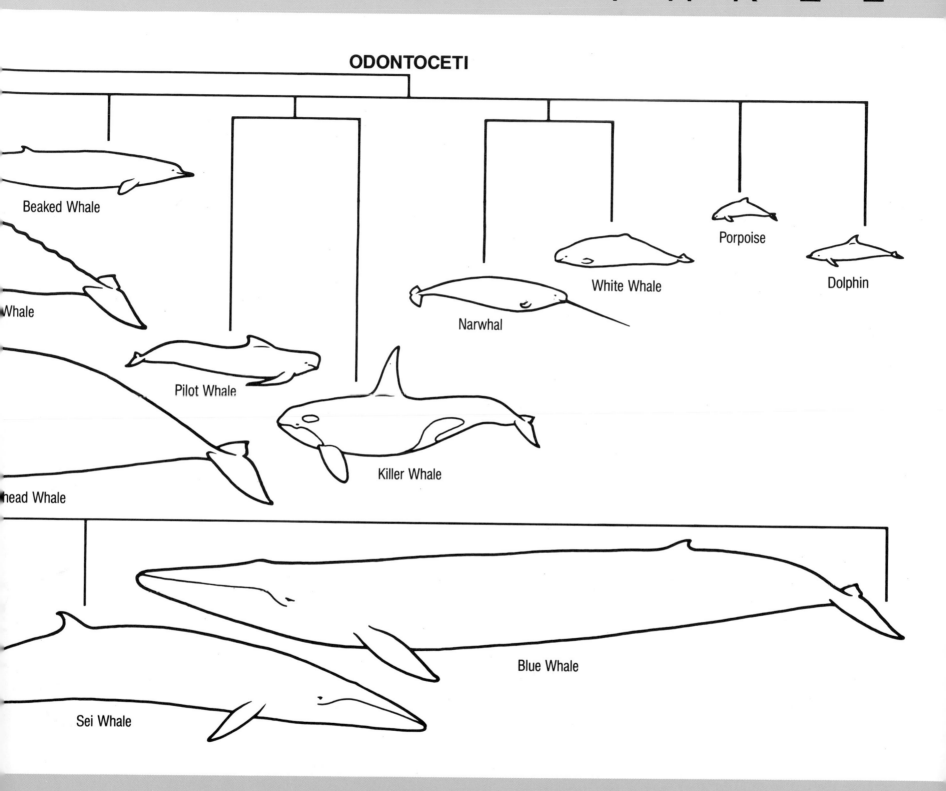

ODONTOCETI

Beaked Whale

Whale

Pilot Whale

Narwhal

White Whale

Porpoise

Dolphin

Killer Whale

head Whale

Sei Whale

Blue Whale

Family Planning

Pieter Folkens' illustrations are noted for their accurate depiction of whale and dolphin characteristics. Here, some living members of the cetacea are shown. (See the chart on pages 30–31.)

The cetacean blood line is comprised of dolphins and porpoises as well as whales and includes at least seventy-seven distinct species. Documented field observations are severely limited so that few specifics are known for distinguishing physical makeup or behavioral patterns. Our knowledge of marine mammals is far from complete; for example, new species of the beaked whale have been identified as recently as the early 1960s. Other cetacean species generate scientific controversy regarding their proper definitions. It seems that many of these marine mammals may be truer representations of subspecies, in particular the wide variety of bottlenose dolphins. But until further inroads are made in the area of taxonomy, such subspecies remain as one classification, subject to geographical variants.

The killer whale (far right) is carnivorous and fully toothed. The open jaw of this California gray whale (right) gives full view to his baleen plates, which he uses to strain his food from the sea.

© Jeff Foott

The Mysticeti

The current order of cetacea is divided into two suborders: the mysticeti and odontoceti. The mysticeti suborder is composed of the baleen whales while the odontoceti suborder (toothed whales) includes sperm whales, beaked whales, monodonts, dolphins, and porpoises. The distinction between whales and dolphins hinges on the size of the species. Those cetaceans that are more than twenty feet long are commonly considered whales. The mysticeti include the family Balaenopteridae comprised of the humpback, blue, fin, sei, Bryde's, and minke (little piked) whales; the family Balaenidae includes the right and bowhead whales; the family Neobalaenidae, the pygmy right whale; and the gray whale, the only member of the Eschrichtidae family. These four families of baleens are distinguished, among other attributes, by the courseness of their baleen, the Balaenidae having fine, long baleen, the Balaenopteridae having coarser baleen, and with the grays possessing the coarsest of the three.

The mysticeti are most often referred to as baleen or whalebone whales. They mature toothless (although the developing fetus starts out with tooth buds), possessing instead a unique feeding device composed of baleen plates. A series of these flattened, rod-like sheets hang from the roof of their mouth much the same as vertical blinds hang in a window. Depending on the individual species, there may be from 200 to 300 individual sheets. However, regardless of the name of "whalebone," baleen plates are neither hard nor structurally rigid. While the outside edge is smooth, the inner side of the plates ends in what appears to be a hairy, fibrous swag frayed at the edges and resembling the bristles on a worn-out paintbrush. To the ancient Greeks, however, it must have looked more like an unkempt, ingrown mustache; mysticeti translates to "mustache-whale." But despite its unimposing, raggedy appearance, its filtering abilities are essential to the baleen whale.

At sea, baleen whales are easily recognizable by their dual blowholes. Some of the larger members may also be identified by a series of folds on the underside of their throats. These stretchable pleats of skin expand, allowing the whale to take in a great amount of water when eating. The baleens who have this characteristic are called rorquals (which means having pleats), a label indicating members of the balaenopteridae family within the mysticeti. There are two subspecies of the rorqual line, but broadly speaking, they may be divided into four general species: the finback, little piked, sei, Bryde's, and blue whales.

Facing page: Krill (top left) usually swim upright, their heads pointed toward the light from above. They propel themselves with their swimmerets (the leg-like structures) and use their tail fins as rudders. The hairy swag of a gray whale's baleen plates (below) clearly indicates why the ancient Greeks named these marine mammals the mysticeti, "the mustache-whale." A feeding whale (far right) uses its long tongue to wipe the baleen plates clean and inverts itself to let the "catch" slide down its throat.

The rorquals are the swiftest among whales, which is astonishing, considering some are also the largest. The normal speed of blue and fin whales is about twelve miles an hour, although in a pinch they can sprint for about twenty minutes at the increased rate of thirty miles (about fifty kilometers) an hour, but the sleekness of the sei whale allows it to maintain thirty-five knots at a clip. Though infrequently hunted because of its smaller size, even harpooned, the sei whale has been known to pull his would-be captor at a sudden rush of forty miles (about sixty-five kilometers) an hour; eventually the intensity of his sprint dies down, but he will continue the struggle at a steady, even pull. They save energy when diving, however, neglecting to hump up (like their larger lookalikes, the blue whales), instead sounding (diving) without flourish, head first into the deep. The exotic food preference of the sei earned them their name, meaning "sardine" in Japanese.

Krill, a small, shrimplike crustacean, no more than five centimeters long (approximately two inches), is the mainstay of the balaenopteridae diet,

© Annette Whelen

© Pieter Folkens

© Jeff Foott

The gray whale, with its dual blow holes, is heavily parasitized with barnacles and lice. The barnacles form white blotches, particularly across his forehead. Although lice is most abundant on his flippers and flukes, it will also fester in open wounds and scars.

and is plentiful in the waters populated by the mysticeti. The whale must consume tremendous quantities at an almost constant rate to sustain his body mass on these tiny morsels. The baleen plates are an ingenious solution. When the whale spots a particularly large patch of krill, he swims right through it, swallowing up greedy gulps in his path. His mouth stocked to its brim with the ocean, he drops his jaw to half mast. Then, pressing his tongue forward to hold back his meal, the whale spits back into the ocean. The matted entanglement of the baleen plates retains the food, while the excess water is expelled between his lips. At carefully chosen intervals, the whale will wipe the baleen clean with his tongue, and invert itself to let the accumulated krill slide down his throat. The whole process requires little energy and the whale bulks up to extraordinary sizes.

Apart from this standard cruising technique, the humpback has developed a second, more active alternative to gathering food. If the krill is too dispersed, the whale may round them up by diving below their most con-

The humpback whale has a series of pleats on the underside of his lower jaw that identify him as a rorqual. These pleats expand when the whale feeds, taking in water along with his catch of krill.

These illustrations by Larry Foster accurately portray the sei whale (above) and the blue whale (right), two of the baleens known as rorquals. The sei are among the fastest swimmers of the rorquals, moving as quickly as thirty-five knots per hour.

centrated level and spiralling up amid the bounty. While twisting, he expels an army of bubbles that concentrate the krill in the eye of his storm. As a result, the whale needs only to angle his mouth upwards to snatch his feast. Feeding is a continuous routine, making this whale the grazer of the sea.

The humpback whale bull is most famous for his melodious moanings, sometimes called "songs," which are the most extended and complex in all of the animal kingdom, and he is notoriously expressive during mating. A newborn calf will have wrinkly skin, resembling the sometimes shriveled appearance of a day-old human infant. The body of the humpback becomes increasingly svelte as you pass over the dorsal hump and fin. His fifty-foot (fifteen meter) frame carries the largest flippers of any cetacean, often growing to a full fourteen feet (four meters) themselves. They are wing-like appendages with delicately scalloped ends. The unique markings on their flukes are as personalized for each humpback as human fingerprints. He is mostly black, but lighter underneath, with large white patches on the ventral surface

© Larry Foster/Earth Views

The blue whale is distinguished by its mammoth size—it is the largest of all whales.

This mixed media illustration by Pieter Folkens (left) depicts the skeletal structure of three suborders of the cetacea. A rorqual, the finback whale (above) has been called "the greyhound of the sea" because of its sleek lines. Even when diving or being pursued by whalers, the finback rarely draws its flukes above the water line.

of his flukes and flippers. There are twenty to forty pleats on his throat; inside, his baleen is a gray-black. The humpback whale has a head pocked with numerous tubercles, each bearing one or two coarse, hair-like bristles. His bumpy appearance is a badge of maturity, as the head knobs and dorsal humps result from tail lashings received from competing bulls of the herd during mating rituals. While the humpback feeds on krill and schooling fish, he has also been known to consume the occasional sea bird.

The balaenidae consume zooplankton, a group of infinitesimal animals found in the oceans and fresh water bodies. The mysticeti style of hunting is nonaggressive, and for the balaenidae even more so as plankton have no real facility for navigating their environment, their congregations flitting about, instead, at the mercy of the water's currents.

The blue whale, another member of the balaenopteridae is the most enormous creature to have ever lived—nearly three times the size of the largest known dinosaur! (In strictly human terms, that means a child could crawl easily through the blue whale's aorta.) But, amazingly, its total girth is less than that of a full size right whale, lending this ocean giant a streamlined appearance. Visually, it is a deceptive comparison, however, because an 85-foot (30-meter) blue whale may expand during feeding, as much as six times its total volume capacity, leaving its pouch, the 80 to 100 ventral grooves that run the length of its throat and chest, holding as much as one thousand tons (nine hundred metric tons) of food and water.

The blue whale's coloring is highly individualized; although primarily an indigo hue, it varies in shade from slate to dark azure. Mottled pigmentation patterns on their backs make them even more distinguishable from one another. In contrast, the edges of the blue whale's long, pointy flippers are marked by white dappling and their baleen is jet black. The snout is broad and flat, nestling into the lower jaws when the mouth is shut. A simple equation makes the blue whale a mainstay of the whaler's catch: one ton (.9 metric tons) of weight per one foot (thirty centimeters) of length. Their preferred habitats are the Arctic and Antarctic and they migrate to the tropics to warm up for the mating season.

The finback whale, most common of the rorquals, is a second in size only to the blue whale. His overall appearance is noticeably lacking in symmetry. The finback's dorsal side is generally dark, while its ventral side is white with more of the light shading concentrated on his right, especially around the head. The left frontal area of his jaw is gray, as are the lower sides of his fins and flippers. The break in coloration that begins on his beak extends to the inside of his mouth as well. The front baleen may be white, while the rest of the plates are always dark gray with streaks of yellow.

The smallest of all the rorquals is the little piked, or minke, whale. It is often mistaken for the toothed killer whale, as both reach a maximum length of thirty feet (nine meters). The baleen of the little piked is yellowish-white and only twelve inches (thirty centimeters) long.

All of the rorquals suffer from a corrosive pitting of the skin along their flanks and tail. These unexplained sores are approximately three inches (seven-and-a-half centimeters) in diameter and one inch (two-and-a-half centimeters) deep. They may appear on captured whales as fresh wounds or scar tissue hollowed from the whale's blubber. At first, their discovery was dismissed as inconsequential, a minor annoyance akin to the human

ight whales (right) are distinguished by white patches on their skin called callosites. These callosites are home to lice and barnacles. Scientists theorize that the callosites may serve as a splash deflector to prevent water from entering the whale's blowhole.

affliction of mosquito bites, but recent hypothesis has suggested they may be the painful souvenirs of shark encounters. Similar abrasions appear on the bodies of various toothed whales, most frequently on the heads and jaws of sperm whales, but these are battle scars from the squid, rather than the shark. The indigestible parts of squid turn up regularly in the stomachs of dissected whales.

With the notable exception of the sperm whale, a member of the odontoceti suborder, the mysticeti suborder have been the most widely hunted. Many within the balaenidae family are now endangered species. The Arctic-dwelling bowhead, for example, now numbers only 2,500. Even though they have been officially protected since 1935, scientists believe they may never fully recover from their brush with extinction.

The smallest of this select group is the pygmy right whale. It is one-third the size of other right whales and, unlike its mates, marked by a dorsal fin. The whalebone in a pygmy is an uneven yellow shade, and not as uniformly

Barnacles are encrusted only on the left side of this female California gray whale (near right). Like humans, gray whales are "right-handed" or "left-handed." Her preference for feeding from the right keeps the right side of her hide free from barnacles. A California gray (far right) breaches off Laguna San Ignacio, in Baja, California. Gray whales breach often, hoisting themselves almost clear of the water, usually landing on their backs.

dense as in others of the suborder. Few habits are known to distinguish them, in part because of their rarity. They are so infrequently sighted that more pygmy whales have been studied as stranded specimens than observed living at sea or in captivity.

One of the first whales to command modern man's attention is a member of the Eschrichtidae family. The gray whale struggled back from near-extinction in the 1950s under the watchful eye of newly aroused cetacean enthusiasts. Officially protected since 1946, the number of gray whales off the North American west coast has stabilized at about 18,000, almost the number that existed in pre-whaling times.

The gray whale resembles both the right whale and the rorqual. However, while the right whale enjoys a prolonged courtship with its partner (far beyond the traditional mating season), gray whales tend to migrate alone. Even their loyalty to the herd is unstable, as the animals often regroup. The cow and calf pairings last only six months.

Unlike the many ventral grooves that extend over half the length of a rorqual's body, the gray whale, forty to forty-six feet (twelve to fourteen meters) long, makes do with only two to five creased pleats, stretching no more than five feet (two meters). This is the cause, or perhaps the result, of a lifetime of finicky eating habits. Because the gray whale likes to take his meals very close to shore, he requires only a small amount of the air supply necessary to most feeding whales. The gray whale maintains a diet based on bottom-dwelling crustaceans called amphipods and shrimp, worms, and crustaceans. He is apt to ingest sand, rocks, and a great deal of other materials unintentionally. In addition, he prefers to feed from the right side of his mouth, evidenced by his whalebone plates, which are worn shorter on the one side, and the scarring (left by bottom-diving) that is found predominately on the right side of his head. His yellowed baleen is made up of unusually thick blades, with 150 to 175 sheets on either side of his mouth.

His mottled, gray hide is distinguished by its heavy encrustation of parasites. The flesh of the gray whale is studded with barnacles—creating a patchwork of white, yellow, and orange embedded with concentrations of whale lice. A low hump takes the place of a dorsal fin, where a series of up to twelve bumps forms a ridge starting at the stock of his tail and running along as far as the flukes.

The whales here and on the facing page are all members of the mesoplodon genus. Though there are many species of this genus, little is known about them and they are often confused with other members of the odontoceti. From top to bottom: Hubb's beaked whale, gingko-toothed beaked whale, and the strap-toothed whale.

© Pieter Folkens

The Odontoceti

The odontoceti, or toothed whales, make up the second suborder of the Cetacea. It is within this classification that we find marine mammals other than the whale. Though commonly called "whales," the sperm, pilot and killer whales, and narwhals and white whales actually are members of three distinct families within the odontoceti suborder: the Physeteridae, the Globicephalidae, and the Monodontidae respectively. River and coastal dolphins, porpoises, and beaked and bottlenose whales comprise the rest of the odontoceti suborder. Besides the absence of the baleen plates, the odontoceti have a melon-shaped forehead and a single blowhole. Diet is less limited and their prey consists of larger animals taken individually.

The bottlenosed and beaked whale are from the family of Ziphidae, the second largest group of cetaceans. They are somewhat related to the sperm whale but are physically more compact, usually between fifteen and thirty feet (between four-and-a-half and nine meters) long. These smaller

Note that mesoplodon foreheads are not as bulbous as those of other beaked whales and the tips of their lower jaws extend slightly beyond the upper jaw. From top to bottom: Blainville's beaked, Gray's beaked, and Andrew's beaked whale.

whales earn their name from the beaked appearance of their snout (which is sharply defined in all of the species) and feast primarily on squid. Often, they are distinguished by highly rounded foreheads, with two deep grooves across their throats that diverge in both directions and come close to meeting in the front. As a rule, bottlenosed whales are spindly, with small flippers that are often pressed into slightly recessive cavities alongside the body. There are at least eighteen of their species, including the northern and southern bottlenose; Sowerby's, Blainville's and Baird's beaked whales; the Tasman or Shepherd's beaked; and the straptoothed and ginkgo-toothed whales.

The northern bottlenose is frequently cited for his gregarious nature. He habitually (and quite fearlessly) greets approaching ships. Norwegians, as well as other whalers who have encountered this host of the cool North Atlantic and deep Arctic waters, have often repaid his gracious overtures with a fatal harpoon. On the other side of the hemisphere, the southern bot-

Five members of the mesoplodon genus from top to bottom: Hector's beaked, Bering Sea beaked whale, Sowerby's beaked, Gervais' beaked, and True's beaked whale.

tlenose shyly evades all passers-by, blessed by a singular lack of curiosity. The bulls of both species have one tooth on each side of the lower jaw. Their long, rounded bodies are brown or gray, usually fading to white or yellow patches around the heads of older males.

The mesoplodon genus represents the strangest of the order of Cetacea, and cetologists know very little about them. Many mesoplodon species have never been seen alive; their existence is documented exclusively through strandings or the fortuitous discovery of bone fragments. Included in this group are the aforementioned beaked whales (excepting the Tasman) along with Andrew's, Hubb's, Gervais', Gray's, Hector's, Stejneger's, Longman's, and True's. Similarly toothed as the northern and southern bottlenose, Sowerby's beaked whale has the dubious distinction of being the most commonly stranded among these whales. From an unfortunate circumstance, Sowerby's whale had the honor of being the first beaked whale ever written about. In 1804, the English watercolorist James Sowerby found

Like mountain rams, male narwhals probably use their tusks to establish a social advantage through physical dominance. Scarring on the foreheads of adult males is a result of dueling.

© Jenny Wardrip

© Gregory Silber/Earth Views

the whale stranded along Moray Firth in Scotland. Its hardy body and slightly bulging forehead is a darkly mottled bluish gray, with a length of about fifteen to seventeen feet (four-and-a-half to six meters).

Baird's beaked whale is the largest member of the Ziphidae family. Japanese biologists have estimated its gestation period at seventeen months, the longest yet for any member of the cetacean order. It dives deeply, submerging for forty-five minutes or more, leaving trackers baffled. Consequently, field studies are difficult endeavors. However, it seems to prefer the offshore temperatures of the North Pacific and travels in herds of up to thirty animals, segregated by sex and blowing in unison. There may be as many as four teeth in the lower jaws of both males and females. However, when their mouths are closed, only two teeth protrude towards the front of the Baird's whale's pointy mouth, creating an illusion of a snowy-tipped beak. They grow up to forty-two feet (thirteen meters) long (the females slightly larger), and their slate gray bodies are traversed by innumerable white scratches.

Blainville's beaked whale sports a world-wide habitat and, as such, an accurate count is unknown, although it is unlikely that the Blainville's are as rare as other beaked whales. The mature male of the species, noted for his pancake forehead and prominent lower jawline, exhibits the more exacting characteristics necessary for proper identification of the herd. The body is gray and blotchy with lighter areas of shading drawing towards the belly. But its most startling characteristics by far are the two large teeth perched on each side of the Blainville's jutting jaw, horn-like in their extension, sometimes rising triumphantly above the creature's head. Richly coated with barnacles, the teeth measure an overall six to eight inches (fifteen to twenty centimeters) in length.

The Tasman beaked whale is nearly impossible to identify at sea, as its outwardly distinguishable traits are quite subtle. It is, however, noteworthy as the only beaked whale with a full set of upper and lower teeth, in addition to the two larger teeth that protrude from the lower jaw of the male alone. Likewise the Ginkgo-toothed beaked whale can claim notoriety (along with his name) just by the shape of his teeth; discovered by Japanese scientists in 1957, the two flattened fangs of the male are said to resemble the fan-shaped leaves of the ginkgo tree. Yet undoubtedly the most bizarre member of this large, diverse family is the straptoothed whale. The female of this unusual species is fourteen to fifteen feet (four-and-a-half meters) long; her male counterpart grows up to nineteen feet (six meters). As with the other beaked whales, there are two teeth in the lower jaw, one projecting on each side. But as he matures, the straptoothed bull's teeth continue to grow until, at thirteen inches (thirty-three centimeters), they curve around the upper jaw preventing the adult male from fully opening his mouth. Scientists have added it to their list of cetacean puzzlements.

Mystery follows the male narwhal, a member of the white whale family called monodontidae. It has a single tooth which extends through its upper lip into a long, twisted tusk; the eruption appears during the first year and at maturity may reach ten feet (three meters). There are two additional teeth lodged in the upper jaw of both sexes. Broken tusks are common and afflict 30 to 40 percent of the adult male whales. Those lucky enough to spot the tusked-whale relate tales of dueling narwhals. This dueling may create scars on the male narwhals.

While it is predominantly a male trait, female narwhals have occasionally sprouted a single tusk, and a small number of males have been documented with two. Its clockwise spiral would seem to be a useful tool for navigating through pack ice of the narwhal's Arctic environment, but that theory has been discounted as observers have documented the male's caution regarding his horny appendage, which leads to speculation that the tusk may instead be a secondary sex characteristic useful in establishing a social hierarchy. When faced with an icy entrapment of no more than six inches in thickness, narwhals open up breathing holes by butting with the bulbous cushion of their fatty foreheads.

Generally, the narwhal is a gray-white with darker, varying smokey shades speckling its back. Smooth and finless, its flippers are rounded back and the extended curvature that ends its flukes appears to be a physical afterthought. In fact, in older males its assembly is so preposterous it appears that the flukes have been tailored backwards.

The beluga whale, relative to the narwhal, remains white throughout adulthood although he is born a bluish-gray. During the five years of adolescence, the white whale may even appear rather yellow. Another Arctic dweller, he much prefers the shallow waters. The chubby beluga averages only four to five miles (six to eight kilometers) an hour. And yet, he can be a most intrepid migrator. Normally spotted in groups of two or three, the belugas find confidence in numbers, assembling herds of hundreds, even thousands, for exploratory jaunts up the northern rivers. They enjoy a wide variety of fish and crustaceans, occasionally tackling the odd octopus. In all, around forty-four conical teeth are set in on both sides of their upper and lower jaws, though some belugas have as few as thirty-two teeth.

The sperm whale is the goliath of the odontoceti suborder, males attaining lengths of fifty to sixty feet (fifteen to eighteen meters). Still he is only about half the length of the blue whale. However, it is the sperm whale that is the most economically significant of all cetacean species. His name refers to the spermaceti found in the cavernous reservoir of his forehead, so called by early whalers who mistakenly believed it was material for mating. Actually, it is a pool of translucent spermaceti oil frequently used in the manufacture of candles and ointments. Fifteen barrels may be extracted from a sin-

revious page: The white beluga whale is perhaps the most gregarious marine mammal. They travel in groups of twenty to two hundred (although a number in the thousands is not unheard of). Their constant chatter prompted early whalers to call them "the sea canaries."

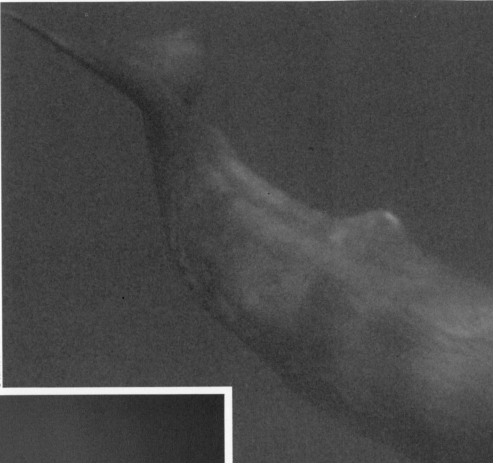

© James D. Watt

© James D. Watt

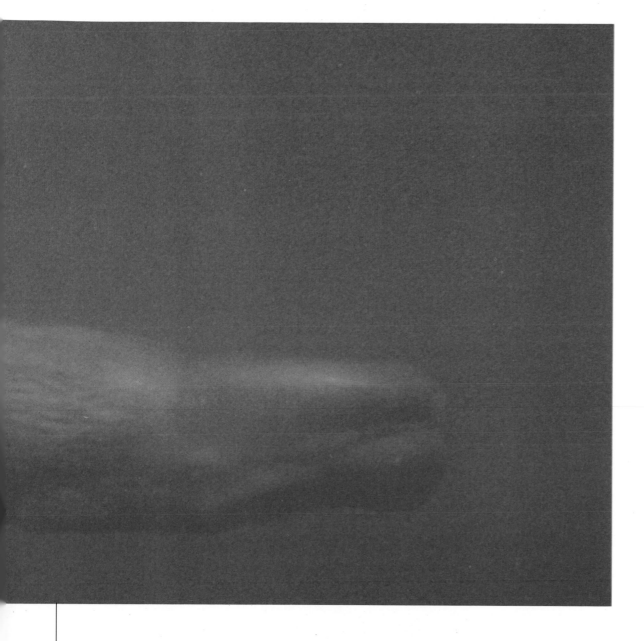

Left: It is believed that a diving sperm whale can reach depths of 10,000 feet (about 3,050 meters) and remain submerged for over an hour. When skimming across the surface, a sperm whale swims with an undulating motion. At top speed his head lifts entirely out of the water and, with his jaw in full view, the head rises and pitches with the rapid beat of his flukes.

gle sperm whale and the thicker wall of its blubber holds an additional supply of other whale oil. The sperm whale also carries ambergris, a waxlike substance useful in producing fine perfumes; literally translated from the French, it means "gray amber." The base is soluble in alcohol and, while imparting a sweetly lingering fragrance, manages to balance the perfume's other ingredients by stabilizing their absorption properties to identical rates of evaporation. Lighter than water, ambergris sometimes washes ashore, usually in small gray, black, or variegated masses. It was historically treasured by alchemists who believed it possessed miraculous healing powers. Ambergris is found within the whale's intestines, likely a byproduct of indigestible beaks left from the cuttlefish, squid, and octopus that are staples of

These killer whales (inset) were sighted off the coast of Vancouver Island in Canada. Although each killer whale (right) is no more than thirty-two feet in length, a pack can bring down the largest blue whale.

the sperm whale's diet. In recent years, the cosmetic industry has replaced ambergris with synthetic copycats.

The sperm whale is nearly all black with deft silver shading across his belly. The surface layer of his skin is deeply creviced, with a prune-like texture. At birth, this wrinkling is concentrated along the throat area furrowed with pleats as in gray whales. But as the sperm whale ages, the condition spreads evenly to envelop the entire mammal. He is toothed in the lower jaw only (with eighteen to twenty-eight conical teeth on each side), but the upper jaw is also marked by tooth-socketing, which permits the mouth to be sealed by sliding the lower teeth into the upper jaw-casings.

Sperm whales are quickly identified at sea by the bushy shaft of their blow, which sails forward towards the left side of the head, due to an irregular blowhole, which rests off-center and is s-shaped. A sounding sperm whale may remain submerged for over an hour and they routinely dive well below 1,500 feet (450 meters). Carcasses of the larger males have been found at

© Jeff Foott

© Jeff Foott

any consider the orca, or killer whale, the smartest species of the cetacea. While a brutal adversary to other marine mammals, they are the super-stars of marine park shows. Here, Shamu goes through the motions at Sea World in Orlando, Florida.

levels of 3,720 feet (one kilometer), trapped into death by entangled submarine cables. It is believed that they may occasionally plunge to depths of 10,000 feet (3,000 meters).

The sperm whale is highly evolved socially and within the herd there are many complex relationships. A male in his prime protects and provides for a harem of ten cows. Younger bulls travel in bachelor herds, road warriors out to establish their own harems. Another group consists entirely of older males who are no longer interested in policing a female bevy. But regardless of their social circle, when the time comes, the males of the herd will migrate en masse to denser feeding grounds while the females remain behind in the breeding waters.

The so-called killer whale (or orca) is really a member of the dolphin family. They are primarily fish eaters, although seals, penguins, and sea lions may also make the menu. (The opened stomach of one twenty-foot (six meter) orca revealed the remains of twelve porpoises, fourteen seals, and six seabirds that were consumed over a period of time.)

The killer whales are skillful pack-hunters (preying on twenty-five known types of whale and dolphin), meticulously choreographing their attacks so that they are able to take down animals more than three times their individual size, which is usually no more than thirty-two feet (nine and a half meters) in length. Orca herds have outmaneuvered even the great blue whale to its final defeat.

An attack on a sperm whale would likely proceed as follows: The individual prey is isolated from the herd by circling orcas. The animal is teased by the pack, which darts at it at once from all angles with quick, threatening motions. Finally, one of them will take firm hold of the sperm whale's tail, effectively slowing down the tiring, panic-stricken creature. As it succumbs to exhaustion, the sperm whale's mouth drops open and his massively engorged tongue slips into the water. Having coaxed it from these giant jaws, the pack strikes as a unit, devouring it along with most of the head. The less desirable portions of the sperm whale's flesh are left behind for other predators, presumably barracuda and sharks.

Killer whales inhabit marine parks and aquariums. As the subject of many scientific studies there, they have been judged as cooperative, curious, and reasonably gentle. However, because they are easy to train in captivity we can't assume they are "friendly" in human terms. Killer whales have been known to attack their trainers and aren't the gentle giants they may appear to be. Many believe the orca are the smartest members of the cetacean order. Although the family to which they belong contains no true whale species, cetologists find that conclusions about the killer whale in some degree apply throughout the suborder, for which reason, further examples of their behavior may be duly noted.

THE WHALE ORDER MEMBERS		SPECIES	ALSO KNOWN AS	DISTINGUISHING FEATURES
THE SUBORDER MYSTICETI (BALEEN WHALES)		BLUE WHALE	Sibbald's Rorqual, Sulphur Bottom	Mottled bluish gray; length: 100 feet (33 meters); weight: 119 tons (108 metric tons); 2 blowholes
		COMMON RORQUAL	Finner Whale, Finback, Razorback	Body light gray above, pure white below; pale chevron sometimes visible on back; length: 82 feet (27 meters); weight: 70 tons (63 metric tons)
		HUMPBACK WHALE	Humpback Whale	Black on black markings with varying white patches on underside; length: 45–50 feet (15-16.5 meters); weight: 40 tons (36 metric tons); (females 2–3 feet [0.6-1 meter] longer than males) numerous tubercles on head
		RIGHT WHALE	Northern, Greenland, Black, or Biscayne Right	Smooth black back, white chin, mottled belly, white and pink callouses on head, horny lump on snout; length: 35–50 feet (11-16.5 meters); weight: to 50 tons (45 metric tons); (females up to 10 feet [3 meters] longer than males)
		PYGMY RIGHT WHALE	Pygmy Right Whale	Length: 15 feet (5 meters) (females up to 6 feet [2 meters] longer); unusually stout skeleton with very broad ribs
		GRAY WHALE	California Gray, Devilfish	Mottled gray, low hump followed by bumpy ridge; length: 40–45 feet (13-15 meters); weight: 20–35 tons (18-32 metric tons); head just over ⅕ total body length
THE SUBORDER ODONTOCETI (TOOTHED WHALES)		SPERM WHALE	Sperm Whale	Nearly all black with silvery shading on belly; length: 60 feet (20 meters) [female is half as long]; no dorsal fin
		BOTTLENOSED WHALES	Beaked, Bottlehead	Closely related to sperm whales; length: 15–30 feet (5-10 meters); snout is beaked with high, rounded forehead; males have 1–2 pairs of teeth exposed in lower jaw only
		NARWHAL	Narwhal Narwal or narval	Gray-white with dark mottling; males have 1 tusk, twisted clockwise in spiral of up to 9 feet [3 meters]; length: 16 feet (5.3 meters) excluding tusk (females slightly smaller); no dorsal fin
		BELUGA	White whale	Pure white coloring; chubby body with enlarged forehead, flexible, defined neck, and flippers that curl at the edges; no dorsal fin

DIET	BREEDING	HABITS OR OTHER STATISTICS	LOCATION	PRESENT STATUS
As much as 4 tons of krill per day in summer	Sexually mature at 10 years; gives birth once every 2–3 years; 12-month gestation; nurses for 8 months	Solitary life; largest animal to ever exist; 50 year longevity; blow lasts 5 minutes, rising to 49 feet (16 meters); speed: 12–14 knots	Worldwide; largest populations in southern hemisphere; migrates to low latitudes for breeding	Endangered; estimated population: 11,200; protected by International Whaling Commission since 1966
Varies with season, including krill, herring, cod, pollock, and capelin	Sexually mature at 8 years; mates in winter; 11–12 month gestation; nurses for 7 months	Travels in herds of 6–7; blow rises to 20 feet (7 meters); remains submerged up to 30 minutes; emits loud, low frequency sounds at 20 Hz with a pitch near the bottom end of human hearing	World-wide with a concentration in southern ocean	Estimated population: 20,000
Krill, schooling fish, occasional bird when lunge-feeding	Pairing and calving in winter; gives birth every 2–3 years; 11–12 month gestation; sometimes nurses beyond first year	Observed in groups of 200 or more in feeding areas; blow rises to 20 feet (7 meters); remains submerged for 20 minutes	Worldwide, but found mainly in coastal waters	Endangered; worldwide protection since 1966; estimated population: 8,000–10,000
Krill and planktonic copepods	Mates in July; 276-day gestation	Migratory	Arctic; near shore in cooler waters of northern hemisphere	Nearly extinct since the 1920s; estimated population: 420; protected but population is not recovering
Possibly copepods	Gestation is probably 10–11 months	Smallest and least known of baleen whales	Inshore shallow waters and protected bays of South America, Australia, and New Zealand	Rare; numbers unknown
Wide variety of invertebrates	Births occur in winter, every 1–3 years; 11–12 month gestation; nurses for 6–9 months	Strong bonding between cow and calf	North Pacific from Japan to California	Protected since 1946; population stabilized at about 16,500
Squid and cuttlefish	365–480 day gestation; mature at 8 years	Hunted for oil in head; source of amergris; may submerge for 70 minutes; blow inclined forward to left side of head, lasts 6 seconds; speed 3–4 knots, increasing to 10–12 if pursued	World-wide	Numbers reducing
Mainly squid	Possible 12-month gestation	Coastal variety travels in herds of 10; offshore type travels in groups of up to 25; cooperative hunters	North Atlantic, Indian Ocean, New Zealand, or Pacific coast of North America	Numbers unknown; presumed rare
Mainly cuttlefish, but also crustaceans, squid, and bottom fish such as halibut	Gives birth mostly in summer; 14–15 month gestation; calves born blueish-gray in color, but change color later	Travels in groups from 3–20, usually sexually segregated	Deep water of the northern Arctic	Overall population unknown, but believed to number 10,000 in Canadian Arctic
A wide variety of fish, crustaceans, and cephalopods	3-year reproductive cycle; sexually mature at 5 to 6 years; gives birth mainly in summer; 14-month gestation nurses for about 20 months	Extensively migratory, but very poor swimmer, typically moving at 5–6 mph; travels in groups of 2 or 3, but in summer forms herds of hundreds, even thousands	Shallow waters of Arctic	Estimated population: 62,000 to 88,000

CHAPTER FOUR

The Intelligent Alien

Members of the mysticeti suborder, like this finback whale, have not evolved the sophisticated brains of their odontoceti counterparts. Finbacks do emit low-frequency sounds, however, leading some scientists to believe that they are some sort of communication signal to others of their species.

Many oceanographers, Jacques Cousteau most prominent among them, question the validity of searching the universe for intelligent life forms without exploring the possibility that they already exist here on our own planet. One determining factor in such expeditions has always been the presence of water on the earth's surface. The sprawling seas of earth once served as the watery womb for life as we know it today. For billions of years, deep in the dark recesses of the ocean floor, DNA, the genetic code, developed and replicated until it matured into all species.

The sperm whale's brain is the largest and most specialized in the mammalian order. However, scientists have had difficulty evaluating its mental capacities. For warm-blooded creatures to survive in the icy ocean, they must develop a means of conserving heat. Whales' inner layer of skin developed the ability to hold great amounts of fat—their blubber replaced the need for hair as an insulator. Whales also maintain a higher metabolic rate than their cold-blooded neighbors. And so begins the whale's biological chain of command: the higher the metabolic rate, the faster the heartbeat and respiratory rate; glandular secretions and bodily excretions must also keep pace; and, above all, there is the increased demand for food so that there will be a sufficient energy base to keep everything functioning at peak. Consequently, the whale cruises along on a steady search for food, moving with great speed. In the case of toothed whales, such a steady hunt

A blue whale skeleton (inset), assembled by the Long Marine Lab at the University of California, Santa Cruz, shows the massive size of the blue's jaw. The killer whale skull (right) offers an imposing view of the killer's razor-sharp teeth.

requires a more highly evolved sensory mechanism, which in turn creates the need for a larger, more specialized brain. The mysticeti on the other hand rely on instinct to migrate to their feeding grounds.

The core of a whale's nervous system, like that of all vertebrates, is protected within the braincase and vertebral column. One of the first examinations of a whole brain specimen was conducted in 1885. The dissection of this fragile organ required optimum delicacy and, yet, the surrounding bone was so resistant, that it took five hours of hard labor just to extricate the brain from the skull. Today, aided by state-of-the-art instruments, it is still a lengthy process, and one of the toughest tasks facing a zoologist.

Visually, the whale's brain bears a striking resemblance to our own. The cerebral cortex is covered with individual convolutions and fissures, which provide an essential criterion for judging the level of brain development. Its complex state indicates a strongly centralized nervous system, which would suggest a stronger motivational, rather than instinctual, dependency on the brain than found in other forms of mammal life. Additionally, the surface structure of the whale's brain is organized in a cellular development pattern not found in other animals. The cortex is thinner than that in comparably large-brained creatures, but the total surface area is greater than it initially appears due to the intricate folding of the fissures. Even in lieu of the whale's enormous body size, it is startling to note that the brain of a sperm whale has been recorded at a weight as high as 19$\frac{1}{2}$ pounds (9 kilograms).

The weight of the cerebellum, the primary control center for all voluntary movement, amounts to as much as 20 percent of the whale's total brain bulk, compared to the 10 percent usually accounted for in the brain of a terrestrial animal. When it is highly developed, as it is in the whale, it endows remarkable agility. The white matter of the whale's cerebellum is more highly ramified (has more fissures) than that of any other mammal, including man. The extensive development of the whale's tactile nerves may allow the whale to sense water pressure and flow, environmental indicators that its body must respond to for survival.

In sensory development, sight is less important than it would be for most mammals. Regardless of the sun's intensity on any given day, 90 percent of white light is absorbed by the upper coastline layers of the ocean's waters; only 1 percent cuts through to twenty fathoms; at 250 fathoms below sea level, visibility is no more than an infinite black wall. So it is not extraordinary to find that the eye and optic nerve of the whale are grossly underdeveloped. Likewise, the olfactory functions may be completely absent from the whale's sensory makeup. None of this handicaps the animal in any way, however, for his environment is better suited to his finely tuned acoustical sense, which allows the odontoceti to locate their prey.

Less is known about the whale's sensitivity to touch, or his perception of pain or heat. The spinal cord would indicate that these abilities are poorly developed, but since whales react pleasurably to caresses from other whales, as well as to occasional human contact, it seems we must be missing a piece of the puzzle.

The sensation of taste may be reduced in whales. The odontoceti (present-day, toothed variety) whales have papillae at the base of their tongues which may be equated with taste buds. But, in fact, the ninth cranial nerve, the control line for gustatory reactions, is not significantly developed. Sadly, the sense of smell, the single human sensory function nearly undetectable in the whale's development, may prove to be his Achilles' heel. Man has vastly altered the sea's real properties, which has caused unimagined peril for the whale, as well as other marine life. The whale has some ability to reject poisonous material indigenous to his environment. Unfamiliar with plastic bottles and hospital gloves that humans dump into the water, the whale is in danger of swallowing lethal waste materials or feeding on their solid remains often encapsulated in scads of seaweed, which block his intestines or puncture his stomach lining.

Our current definition of intelligence relies on the principles of variant behavior, the ability to recognize causal relationships. As beings who live independently of our environment, we developed ways to survive. Early humans, for example, discovered that fire and clothing themselves would keep them warm. Needing protection from the elements, we developed the tools to build adequate shelter. We also define intelligence by our ability to communicate both verbally and through written language with which we record our history and ideas. Some scientists argue that defining intelligence by these uniquely human characteristics eliminates the classification of all but the fully manipulative, digited animals. By these standards, marine mammals certainly are not "intelligent." However, the whale has shown an adaptability to its environment that exhibits much more than merely "animal" instinct. How then should we define this mammal's "intelligence"?

A meaningful measure of the whale's intellect might include the ability to analyze and associate stimuli with behavior modification, to deliberate and find the means of reaching a desired goal, to imagine the results of a contemplated course of action, and to perceive the concept of continuity, recognizing the relationship of cause and effect. These principles of variant behavior, unlike instinctual activity, are not found among animal groups functioning within more primitive thinking patterns.

Behaviorally, many members of the whale family have exhibited neotenic traits. "Neoteny" is the process by which an animal develops in such a way that its fixed muscular responses and instincts are never completely locked into the adult stage. By retaining certain positive qualities of the juvenile, an animal may manifest the inquisitive disposition necessary for its mind to continually evolve. Physically, this provides the whale with a greater range of flexibility and combined responses, both in determining the sequence of muscle contractions and in matching these contractions to incoming stimuli. The result is an individual creature whose behavior in any given circumstance is neither rigid nor stereotypical; the whale has freedom of choice. And so he must also have the ability to "think," at least in terms of learning through the repetition of experiences.

Unfortunately, though, using a strictly behavioral criterion for evaluating the whale's mind has some notable drawbacks, one of which is that the whale's behavior is variable. For example, the killer whale has been known, in some oceans, to cavort peacefully with the playful sea lions; in other waters, the same killer whale might make a meal of them. On the surface, this would appear to be highly erratic behavior. However, it is possible we are missing some key element and are incapable of predicting their behavior.

Different types of whales demonstrate different methods for fulfilling their

The eye and optic nerve of the whale (above) is poorly developed even though this young gray whale's open eye may seem alert. Odontoceti whales have adapted an advanced sonar-like ability called echolocation to compensate for their poor eyesight.

Gray whales in California are sighted often (below) and sometimes allow humans to touch their highly sensitive hides, which allow the whale to sense both water pressure and the current's flow.

Though this killer whale may appear docile and playful in captivity (right), they have been known to attack their trainers.

© Robert & Linda Mitchell

© Messer Schmidt/FPG International

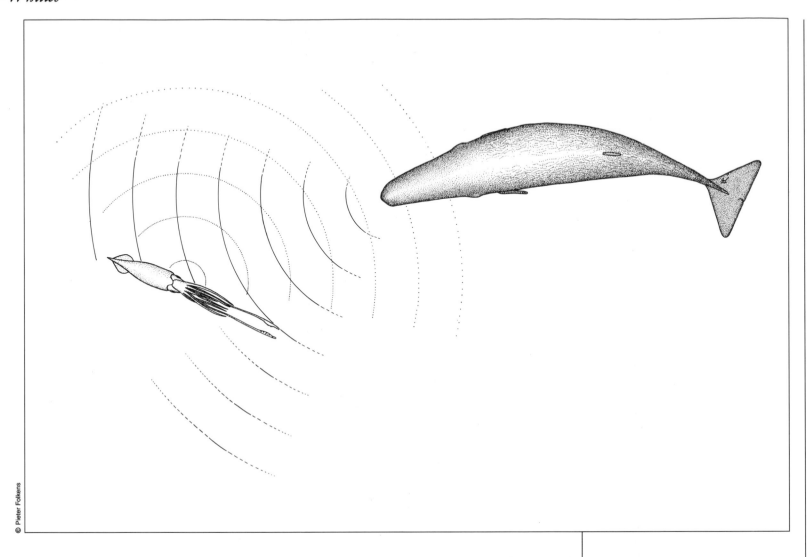

© Pieter Folkens

own needs and have adapted distinct characteristics to meet them. The only characteristic all whales have in common are their locomotive traits: the horizontal flukes and the flipper for steering. The major distinction between the mysticeti and odontoceti are their specialized adaptations for foraging. The mysticeti have not developed a sophisticated social order because their feeding habits are nonaggressive. The odontoceti have adapted highly developed tools for foraging. Just as humans first learned to gather in groups to hunt the mastodon, so the odontoceti developed sophisticated brains and a social order to hunt in herds. To facilitate this, they developed echolocation, a means for communication: they use the balloon-like sacs on their foreheads to create sounds and their lower jaws are filled with an oil that is used as an acoustic receptor. Echolocation is a radar-like system that, for dolphins, is ten times more accurate than our most sophisticated sonar equipment.

With a little luck, a little more time, and a whole lot of planning, you may be

Odontocetes have developed a highly sophisticated imaging system known as echolocation. Oil in the odontocetes' lower jaws acts as an acoustic receptor, receiving the bioacoustic waves that bounce off objects.

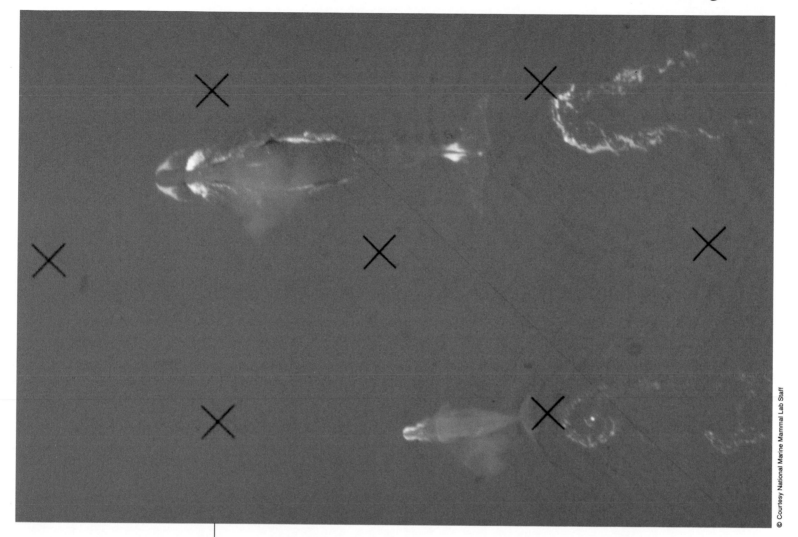

rctic-dwelling bowhead whales are among the most endangered species of whale. With their tough skulls they create cracks in the ice, allowing them to breathe in the Arctic's frozen waters.

fortunate enough to sight a whale. But what you'll actually see may be very slight indeed, as these free-spirited divers cloak themselves in the ocean, pricking the surface on whim with a teasing glimpse as they skim along towards their destination. To study them properly, scientists require some point of access where a herd may be observed residing openly. And the observation of this same herd must consist of an unabated length of time. Such opportunities are rare.

It would seem unlikely that across centuries of development, the whale—an animal which propels itself through the water with the force of a single, primary appendage, would require a more highly developed brain than the many land-based creatures who depend on four limbs to climb and scurry about. Clearly the whale's intellect must be judged by its own abilities, exclusively of humans. As the noted undersea explorer Jacques Cousteau once said, our greatest confusion might be lifted by simply accepting that the whale may be "gifted with senses we have lost or never attained."

CHAPTER FIVE

Mating and Motherhood

The flippers of the humpback whale are longer than those of any other whale, and can grow to as much as one third of their body length. The flippers' delicately scalloped edges and graceful movements have earned the humpback the nickname of "wings on the water." Female humpbacks give birth about every two years, with a gestation period of one year.

For the most part, whales are perfect role models of parental care and training, and enthusiastic lovers as well.

A mating scene of right whales, recorded by Jacques Cousteau, unfolds like this: The female, pursued by two ardent suitors, rolls her white belly up in the creamy ocean waves, the water churned to foam by the undulations of her own body. The males surface upright alongside; one to her left and the other to her right. With their broad fins extended, they compete for her attentions with caressing full-body strokes. Finally aroused, she rolls in submission, although she makes no attempt at selecting her first mate; that is to be determined between the bulls. The two rivals butt heads, shoving and scratching each other on their speckled brows, chalked with the barnacles and lice that distinguishes their species. As their ritualized, controlled aggression continues, they too become fully aroused. The male's reproductive organ extends to five feet (150 centimeters). One of them will recognize the other as victor, and the winning bull will return to the nearby female, mounting her from just below the surface. The female will remain visibly upright on the water, breathing quietly, while the male beneath her remains on his back, and enters her, holding his breath. After a brief eight seconds, he will disengage from his partner and rise for air. One deep invigorating breath and the male will dive again, picking up the seduction where he left off. These couplings may last for hours. Meanwhile, the rejected suitor swims frenzied circles close by, eagerly awaiting his turn.

This is just one of the right whales' methods of lovemaking. He clearly craves intimacy as he swims in herds, exhibiting a persistent need to rub up gently against his companions, regardless of their sex, a form of mild sex play particularly noted in the young who have yet to experience their first mating season. Humpbacks give their lovers playful slaps throughout the mating act, while across the line of species, there is always an occasional bull fond of love bites directed at the flukes of his intended. Still others prefer to vocalize their passion with a reprise of sighs, grunts, moans, and moos.

Some whales mate facing each other in a chest to chest position. The pectoral fins protrude above the water, often crossing over each other as if they were holding hands or entwined in each other's stubby "arms"; their flukes are submerged and pointing downward. Sperm whales in this position can only mate for a matter of seconds as the couple must leap from the

When born, a gray whale calf is fifteen feet (five meters) long and will grow to a full length of about forty-two feet (fourteen meters). Gray mothers are known for aggressively defending their calfs (right).

© Robert & Linda Mitchell

water to remain vertical. As they disengage, they breach in spontaneous joy. In other instances, after a moment of foreplay, whales will dive and swim towards each other at great speed only to surface horizontally, meeting belly to belly on their sides. Here, too, they slide back to sea with a resounding whack after mating for less than a minute.

Whales, as a whole, are notoriously promiscuous. It is not unusual for some to mate with two partners within an hour. The female may reject a potential partner by purposefully floating on her back; or she may flirt with several nearby bulls by pitching herself in the same position, but doing so by a subtle splashy flip. Sometimes the bulls will try to push her back down into position by overriding her on the water. Eventually, though, she must right herself to breathe. So the seduction is inevitable and her antics are merely a coy waiting game. Nevertheless, when a female is ready to accept a partner, they come together with a tenderness that belies their lumbering girth, appearing even to hug each other with their massive flippers.

I n this rare photograph, a gray male penis is exposed as he turns on his side during mating (below left).

© Walt Anderson

It's easy to see why this gray whale's penis (above) is affectionately referred to as "Pink Floyd." Belugas (below) are slate gray to pinkish brown at birth, becoming blue or bluish gray as they mature. Many belugas become completely white in adulthood. The gestation period for belugas is fourteen months and calfs remain with their mothers for as long as two years.

© Pieter Folkens

© Ken Balcomb/Earth Views

Despite their lingering delight in sensual splendor, the right whales seem to follow a doctrine that admonishes the whale to keep its sexual appetite in its proper place. And, surprisingly enough, that means "not in front of the children." They divide their territory between nursery and mating ground, with one area populated exclusively by mothers and their calves; the other with grown males in pursuit of available females.

There is little else in the way of definitive information regarding the whale's sex life. The physiology of the whale's reproductive organs has made learning about their mating patterns difficult. Serious research on cetacean reproduction began at the start of the twentieth century, primarily geared towards setting yearly kill figures that would sidestep the species' annihilation by allowing them to keep a birthing pace. More of this material has been garnered through dissection and biological supposition than through observation of whale behavior. Using this approach, however, scientists have found the sheer size of the cetacea and its reproductive organs a nuisance.

Killer whales are about six feet (two meters) long at birth and weigh about 400 pounds (180 kilograms), and stay with their mothers for at least one year.

The male's testes are held deep within the body, possibly as a streamlining device, but also to protect them from the extreme climactic fluctuations of the water and to sustain the sperm at normal body temperatures. In the blue whales, they may be more than two-and-one-half-feet (seventy-five centimeters) long and weighing, in total, one hundred pounds (thirty-seven kilograms). These two cylindrical organs are burrowed inside the abdominal cavity, behind the intestines and hanging lateral with the kidney. The internal structure of the testes themselves is no different from that of other mammals. While small quantities of semen may be present throughout the year, its production picks up considerably during mating season. In contrast to the size of its organ, whale spermatozoa is identical in size to man's.

At rest, the cetacean penis is completely concealed beneath the abdominal skin; when so retracted, the flaccid organ forms an s-shape within its containment. It is textured like a thin, hard rope. (And in fact, the pizzle or bull whip, formerly used for flogging mutinous sailors, was made from the male whale's organ.) Unlike the human male, it becomes erect not so much through an influx of blood (although a large supply is present here), but through the elasticity of tough connective tissue. The penile base consists of two arms that are fused to the pelvic bones. In the enormous rorquals, the penis may be as long as ten feet (three meters) with a one-foot (thirty-centimeter) diameter. A posterior slit, just below the navel depression, allows for the organ to be pushed outside or drawn within the body by a pair of strap-like muscles found on either side.

The female organs are contained in an elongated genital slit. Smooth, with fine longitudinal folds on the exterior, its interior canal appears to be funneled with a successive chain of folds leading to the cervix. This is a unique development, not present in any other mammals. Their exact function is not known. However, it is possible that they protect the womb from the forces of invading water. It is equally probable that they serve to provide a protective annex for the heavy fetus of a baby whale.

The female's ovaries are housed in roughly the same body cavity as the male's testes, although they are much smaller. A rorqual's ovaries can be up to one-foot-long (thirty-centimeters-long), weighing twenty-two pounds (ten kilograms). While the odontoceti whales have ovaries that resemble those of other mammals, those of the mysticetes bear a closer resemblance to that of birds.

When it was born, this humpback calf was about fifteen feet (five meters) long. When it is fully weaned (after about eleven months), it will be between twenty-four and twenty-seven feet (eight and nine meters) long.

© Ed Robinson/Tom Stack & Associates

When fully grown, humpbacks are as long as forty-eight feet (sixteen meters), though they can be sexually mature when they are only thirty-six feet (twelve meters) long.

The activities of the mating season are taxing on the bull's energies. Likewise, lactation is a demanding process for the cow. And perhaps most traumatic of all is the weaning period for a new calf. The mating season follows a period of feasting at the poles when the females are pregnant. The rorqual females then head to the tropics; lactation ensues ten to twelve months later and the female draws substantially against the fat she stored in her summer at the poles; the males then follow the females to the tropics for mating; finally, the calves wean at the poles, where the food supply is richly abundant. The correlation between this cycle of reproduction and harvest of plenty is best shown by comparing gestation periods among the species. Each has its own distinct rate of fetal growth, allowing for a 4,000-pound (1,800 kilogram) baby blue whale and a twelve-pound (five kilogram) newborn porpoise both to be born in a span of ten to eleven months. A more detailed analysis of the food supply may someday explain why the sperm whale requires such a drawn out pregnancy of a year and four months!

In the final stage of her pregnancy, the mysticeti cow becomes increasingly aloof, avoiding any unnecessary contact with other whales. The variations in her movement are pared down until, on the day of delivery, she stops eating. The cow continues to swim as she goes into labor, but her pace is slowed. Members of the odontoceti suborder, on the other hand, calve in the company of "midwives." The other cows in the herd sense what is about to take place and encircle the cow in labor protectively. A birthing cow is never abandoned by her herd and they will attack to protect her.

Breech births are normal for cetacea; that is quite unexpected for a mammal that delivers a single large offspring. The tail of the newborn emerges first and, as his mother spirals furtively in the water, he will slip out rather suddenly.

The placental tissue in a pregnant whale is exceedingly different from that of a pregnant woman. In the female cetacea, the maternal and fetal tissues are not fused, so that each life maintains their separate vascular structure. Despite the bulk of her newborn, the mother whale loses very little blood in delivery. The flukes of her calf descend cloaked in the smallest pouf of red billows and little more remains of the squat umbilical cord.

Needless to say, the infant whale is no small bundle. Newly born blue whales may be twenty-five feet (eight meters) long and weigh more than two tons (one and a half metric tons); baby fin whales are twenty feet (six meters) and over 4,000 pounds (1,800 kilograms); grays are fifteen feet (four and a half meters), 1,500 pounds (800 kilograms); and the sei, humpback, and sperm whales arrive at fifteen, sixteen and fourteen (four and a half, five, and four meters) feet respectively. This represents a birth size corresponding to 30 percent of their mother's adult body length for mysticete whales and 45 percent for odoncetes.

Whales are born fully developed. Contrary to our lingering childhood development, the cetacean newborn will soon be self-sufficient. Unlike the stumbling calves of terrestrial animals, or our own crawling infants, the baby whale is immediately adept at moving through his environment, swimming beside the female as soon as he's free of the womb. Although he is far from helpless, the newborn is the focus of much concern among the odontoceti herd. The touching warmth and nurturing affection demonstrated between the parent whales at conception is repeated for the benefit of their

© Frank S. Balthis/Nature's Design

Pilot whale calfs (center) stay with their mothers longer than most species of the cetacea, nursing for almost two years. Female pilot whales reach sexual maturity when they are six years old and males reach maturity at twelve years. Gray whales (below) reach sexual maturity between five and eleven years of age when they reach their full size of approximately forty-two feet (fourteen meters).

© Frank S. Balthis/Nature's Design

The mottled gray coloring of these gray whales indicates that they have reached adulthood.

offspring. And this is not a gift exclusive to the realm of the doting mother. Other adult females in the herd will pay close attention to the infant whale's well-being, assisting the mother whenever possible. In fact, there is usually one special "aunt" within the group that the mother whale chooses to grant particularly close contact with her calf from the moment of birth. But first, the new arrival will be escorted to the surface, gently prodded along by the maternal whale. If the newborn fails to surface within ten seconds of his arrival, the lack of air in his lungs may cause him to sink. (Instinctively, the female will push even her stillborn calves up out of the ocean, perhaps believing this will revive them.) As his blowhole crests upon the water, the baby whale inhales his first breath of air. Observers have noted that sometimes mother's female companions tag along—although it is unknown whether this is for emotional support, a celebratory ritual, or simply busybody behavior.

Infant whales feed on mother's milk within an hour of birth. A whale's

© Walt Anderson

mammary glands do not protrude like breasts or udders. Its teats rest in grooves alongside the vulva. Unlike the human newborn, or even other mammalian species, the baby whale does not, in the true sense of the word, suckle. Instead, the milk is squirted down its throat by specialized, contracting muscles that surround the mother's mammary glands. The nursing cow will usually turn on her side so that the calf can feed, swimming to the surface intermittantly for air.

While the newborn instinctually knows his part in the nursing process, for the maternal whale this is most likely a technique learned through the observation of other calving females in the herd. Killer whales have been in captivity for over twenty years, and yet, throughout most of those years, not a single calf born has survived more than a few weeks. The mother orcas refused to allow them access to the mammaries and cetologists were unable to concoct a suitable substitute for mother's milk. When, in 1985, eight-year-old Kandu at the Sea World facility became pregnant, zoologists

When young, gray whale calfs usually are more uniformly dark than their older relatives.

At birth, pilot whales are only six feet (two meters) long and weigh 160 pounds (eighty kilograms). As adults, males will reach a length of eighteen feet (six meters) and weigh three tons, with females growing to a slightly smaller size.

at the marine park embarked on a "parenting program" in the hopes of changing the fate of her growing fetus. By enlisting the aid of other captive whales, they conditioned Kandu's maternal responses—in effect teaching her to accept mammary stimulation as a pleasurable experience. Daily, another adult killer whale would approach the mother-to-be to rhythmically stroke her underside. For her trainers, the months of calculated behavior paid off; while Kandu kept her distance until her afterbirth pains had subsided, several hours after the arrival of Shamu, a female calf, she began nursing. Shamu remains the only killer whale born in captivity to survive and mature.

The amount of time a newborn spends dependent on mother's milk varies between the mysticeti and odontoceti. Mysticeti calves leave their mothers after six months while odontoceti calves will stay with their mothers for as long as six years. While a human mother nurses perhaps four hours a day, the maternal whale offers highly concentrated sustenance; her milk is a rich, thick cream. This allows for shorter feeding sessions, usually no longer than fifteen minutes each day. It also assures the rapid development of fat layers necessary to insulate the young whale from the penetrating cold of the ocean waters. In three short months, the new-born will triple in size.

During those first months of life, the whale calf seldom strays beyond the comforting side of his mother. Sometimes he swims cradled closely beneath her body; other times he leaps playfully across her back, hitching a ride between her fins. When she naps, he'll snooze sheltered by her tail. Soon he will learn that growing up is sometimes fraught with harsh adjustments. His first attempts at adult cuisine often end in vomiting. But mother will be there to rub his belly consolingly with her snout. Maternal whales are devoted to their offspring and exhibit infinite patience as the calf matures, becoming increasingly rambunctious as it nears adulthood. The pre-adolescent whale will bump and butt the cow, testing the limits of his independence as well as seeking the occasional reassurance that is a mother's specialty. In turn, she will respond lovingly, holding him across her chest, hugging and patting his young body. Or, she will snap his tail back with her mighty flipper, clamping him down until he behaves himself.

A humpback whale and her calf swim in the ocean off the coast of Maui (overleaf).

The female's devotion to her young has often been used against her. Unscrupulous whalers have been known to attack a wandering calf to draw out the more highly prized adult whale. This can prove to be a deadly game, not just from the whale's viewpoint. Early whalers often lost their ships, and some their lives, at the rage of a defensive mother. There are many reports of mother and child remaining together, even after one of them has died. Should the mother alone survive, she will diligently defend her calf's carcass from scavenging animals.

Orca herds are matriarchal and consist only of female killer whales and offspring of both sexes, provided they are under two years of age. Usually, only one cow in the herd will bear a calf at a time. The baby killer whale will be born without teeth and, like a human infant, will look for something to teethe on as the sharp new incisors cut through his gums. At first, he'll try his mother's fins, but she'll quickly redirect his attentions, teaching him instead to use his own tongue as a pacifier.

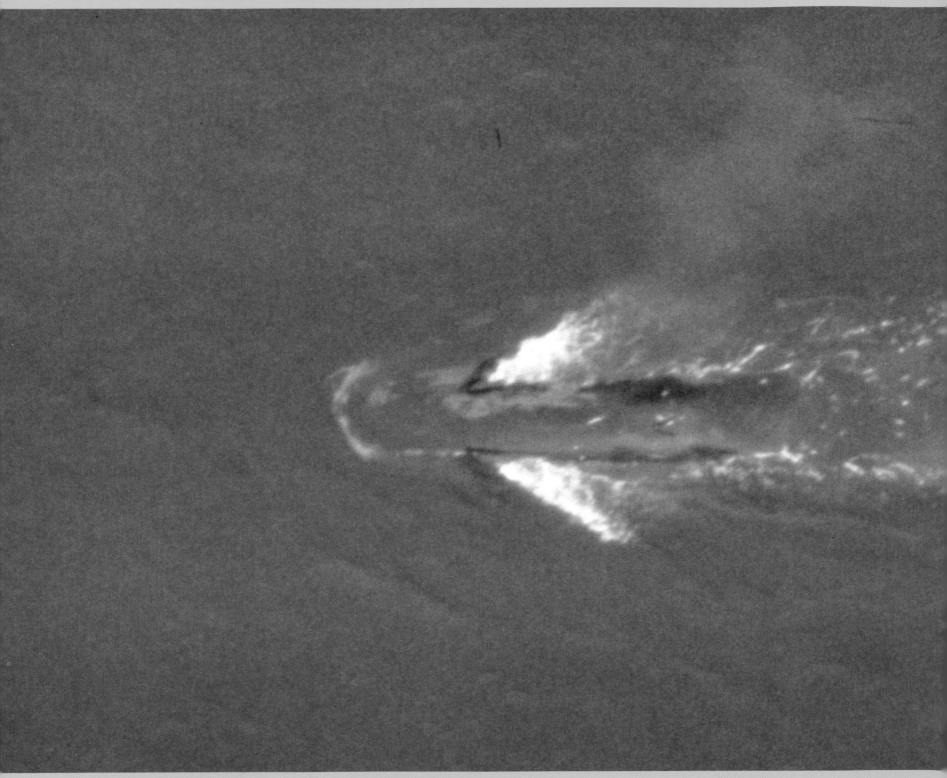

Mysteries of the Migrating Minstrels

U ntil recently, only sporadic information was available on the migration of whales; enough to assure it takes place, but not conclusive enough to determine specifics regarding the routes of different animals and the location of their breeding grounds. The whalehunts of yesteryear have thinned out the herds so that spotting migrational trends is not simple. It is believed that several breeds have altered their journey and established new breeding waters well removed from the ocean's most-traveled shipping lanes. Again the whale's social temperament is a factor; they are difficult to observe at sea, so determining whether a traveling herd is the movement of a family or merely the mutual decision of random individuals is a guessing-game at best.

The study of migrational patterns has been most revealing when the herd travels within sighting of the coastline. Therefore, most of the documentation applies to humpback, right, and gray whales since these whales travel close to shore. Additionally, the migration habits of these whales adhere to a more definite and purposeful outline; they will focus their time and travel exclusively on either food or sex. Summers are spent in polar waters, languidly gorging themselves on unlimited supplies of planktonic crustaceans and mollusks. But soon, the food supply dwindles as the plankton stop reproducing from lack of light as winter approaches, a sign to the whales that the next cycle has begun. The herd will retreat to warmer climates, but the tropical seas present fewer feeding opportunities, so the whale must be prepared to live off the acquired blubber of his polar feasting. The winter courtship is served up with much aplomb. And relocation to warmer waters is a welcome relief to the immature calves who have yet to develop the climate control achieved by years of insulatory fat. The speed with which they migrate also corresponds to a life cycle. The whales arrive in the tropics just in time to give birth and return to the pole as the ice begins to melt. Accordingly, nursing cows are the last to move south and the first to move north, permitting them the shortest stay in frigid waters.

Throughout the long journey, separate, distinct populations of the same species have been noted as well. Humpback whales of the southern hemisphere have been clearly divided into six groups, each migrating within its own fairly restricted zone.

For example, come October, the gray whales will leave their feeding

© Marc Webber/Earthviews

Sperm whales mate and calve in temperate, tropical waters. Females remain in these waters all year long, while the males migrate to the polar regions to feed after the eight-month breeding season.

Summer
Feeding Grounds

Southern Winter Migration Route

Northern Summer Migration Route

Winter
Mating and Calving
Grounds

© Jeff Foott

© Robert & Linda Mitchell

The flukes of a gray whale break the horizon (above and below left). The gray whale migrates 5,000 miles (about 8,000 kilometers) from its Arctic feeding grounds in summer to the bays and lagoons of Baja, California, in winter to mate. Calves conceived the previous winter are born in these winter-habitat bays and lagoons.

grounds in the Bering Sea and make their way down the expansive shore-line to Baja California for mating and calving. It is a roundtrip of over 9,000 miles (15,000 kilometers), one of the longest migrations of any mammal. The return begins in late March or early April, this time accompanied by the foundling whales. Across the Pacific, another group of grays will be leaving the Korean shores, swimming up the Gulf of Tartary, and finally settling in the Sea of Okhotsk where they feast in isolation.

Sailors have compared the humpback's musical musings to the moans of drowning men, and there is certainly an "otherworldly" quality to his song. But perhaps Ken Norris, a marine sciences professor at the University of California at Santa Cruz describes it best as "animal jazz," a syncopated progression of clicks, grunts, sighs, and whistles.

Only the males are singers and it appears that they serenade exclusively for the mating season. They may intend to attract females or to intimidate other males. Or perhaps they are a means of communicating up to thirty miles (fifty kilometers) underwater the activities or whereabouts of an indi-

vidual. However, this remarkable ability may be more of an elemental factor than a whale attribute, since water conducts sound waves with considerably more efficiency than air. Nevertheless, at close range, the songs may be felt as well as heard. The sheer force of its power vibrates through the chest of divers and penetrates the hull of passing ships. Each verse may last from fifteen to thirty minutes. Throughout the ensemble, various themes (a series of sequential sounds) will be repeated any number of times. However, regardless of the number of repetitions, the order in which they are performed must stay consistent for one season. The bulls of each territory sing the same song while herds of the same species but in a different geographical region will have a song of their own. While it may seem quite astounding that their memory patterns hold the same sequence of sounds, it is not a locked-in response. When they return to their breeding grounds the following year, the song will have been changed; still, every bull will know its tune. It will consistently display some of last year's variations, yet there will be themes that have never been heard before.

While the songs themselves may be love calls, sporadic, less structured vocalization serves other purposes. Whales exist in a world of overwhelming darkness. Because of this, their acoustic sense augments their limited vision. Sounds in the air are probably difficult for them to grasp. A whale can see no further underwater than a bird can peer through the foliage of his environment.

Early on, the young killer whale is instructed in song by his mother. He will vocalize by carefully contracting and expanding sacs that surround the melon, making high-pitched snorts similar to the noise of air escaping from a balloon.

Right whales are less distinguished singers, limited mostly to low frequency belching punctuated by a tremendous bellow. They often send long, complicated messages of doleful monotony.

Pilot whales squeak and click to communicate; their sound is called echolocation. Like sonar, it is used to locate objects and scan the terrain.

Studies have indicated that the range of clicks are of a pitch and duration unique to one sperm whale, giving each animal an individual voice. It is possible members of the herd may be able to identify each other in this manner. Therefore, the repetition of like sounds may be no more than a tracking device that keeps the herd together.

A gray whale begins to breach in the waters off Baja, Mexico, in Scammon's Lagoon. The Mexican government has declared the lagoon a whale sanctuary where they are even protected from intruding tourist boats.

The Lure of the Shore

A stranded pilot whale is found on the Cape Cod shore. Scientists believe that when geomagnetic aberrations of the shore confuse the whales' bio-acoustic echolocation system.

The beached whale is a hunkering mass of vulnerable flesh caught between death's door and the sea of life. Nobody really knows what causes these intelligent creatures to go to the shore. Perhaps shore erosion confuses the marine mammal's echolocation mechanism. The geomagnetic changes in the shore confuse the whale's biomagnetic echolocation system. There is even a theory of instinctual suicide, with the failure of a herd leader to detect shallow waters leading to the lemming-like deaths of his followers who swim blindly to their peril.

What is known is that all herds in the animal kingdom, including humans, may sometimes be struck by a wave of sudden, uncontrollable panic, not unlike an anxiety attack. On land, cattle have been known to race across fields and down into crippling gorges or drowning rivers in a fit of blind fear. Similarly inconsistent behavior has led to the mass stranding of scores of cetaceans on beaches all over the world.

Whale strandings have been historically documented, particularly strandings of killer whales, false whales, and pilot whales. In Britain, a log of

such strandings has been maintained since the end of the nineteenth century. Sociologists hypothesize that some shoreline settlements were created spontaneously by early settlers eager to take advantage of the many uses of a beached whale carcass.

From 1927 to 1936, over 700 false killer whales were lost in recorded cases of mass strandings, from coastal points in Scotland to Ceylon, Britain to Zanzibar and the Darling District of South Africa. In 1955, sixty-seven pilot whales beached at Westray (Orkneys). It was widely reported that the event followed a panic attack that drove the animals into spasmodic fits of movement, during which they seriously wounded one another.

The mystery casts its shadow on the sperm whale as well. An early record of strandings occurred in 1784, when thirty-two of the great beasts beached themselves in South Brittany. Two strandings occurred within fourteen days of each other off La Paz, on the Gulf of California; twenty-four sperm whales were followed to shore by thirty-four more of their species.

Of course, the explanation could be simply that their panic is set off by the realization that they have placed themselves in shallow water, wherein the ensuing frenzy of their movements casts them towards shore. However, too often attempts to save them are frustrated by the whales' seemingly intense motivational drive to place themselves in certain jeopardy. Both killer and pilot rescue attempts have ended in the animals' return to the shore soon after some of them had been successfully driven back to the sea. It's as if they have reconciled themselves to the fate of their herd, almost as if they have made a suicide pact. Naturalists have even supposed that this is nature's way of safeguarding the waters against the overpopulation of predators.

While the reasons may be debatable, the direct cause of death is clearly defined. Without the support of a surrounding mass of water, the whale's own body weight presses down on his ribs, making his natural breathing process more and more difficult. The animal is likely to become overheated because of the lack of water. As the tide returns to shore, the stranded whale will drown as soon as the waves have swelled enough to cover his blowhole.

Unlike the other species mentioned, gray whales can apparently survive strandings. Occasionally, they will get run aground when caught by a change of tide, only to float free later.

The skeletal remains of stranded whales (left) litter the shore of "Bone Beach" on the coast of Newfoundland, Canada.

Gray whales (right) sometimes run aground when caught in a tide, and float free later. This gray whale was not so fortunate.

© Jeff Foott/Tom Stack & Associates

A gray whale, fatally tangled in fishing gear, makes a fleshy feast for scavenging birds. Whales often are caught in plastic netting which impedes their movement, tires them, and eventually kills them. Many scientists believe plastic—both fishing nets and waste dumped in the sea by humans—is one of the most serious threats to marine life. Hundreds of whales, dolphins, and porpoises are killed or maimed annually from becoming caught in or ingesting plastic.

California grays exhibit such behavior when under attack by killer whales. While they often have the good sense to bid a hasty retreat into the bays, occasionally they become so disoriented with fear that they openly display themselves as a submissive meal—floating belly up, their extended flippers about helplessly. Belugas behave in very much the same way at the approach of killers, though they keep their posture and do not roll over. While they may seem too paralyzed to swim away, belugas are consciously opting for another strategy. In a rather wily defensive maneuver, their stillness helps them elude their predator, who often fails to sense their presence in the water without the sound of fearful thrashing or who may mistake the white beluga for an iceberg.

Many of the more recent strandings of both whales and dolphins are probably the result of disease or instinctual behavior set awry by environmental factors. From the perspective of the marine biologist, each stranding is an important opportunity to collect data. Tissue samples are extracted from

© David Makris

This humpback whale, washed up on the shores of Truro, Massachusetts, was a victim of "red tide." Little is known about the organism that causes red tide, which lives in the ocean undetected until its numbers suddenly swell enough to tint the shoreline waters red. It is believed that red tide depletes the water's oxygen content and systematically asphyxiates plant and animal life nearby.

these animals for studies on both human and marine mammal health problems.

The Marine Mammal Stranding Network was instituted following the Marine Mammal Protection Act of 1972 and the Endangered Species Act of 1973. It is organized through the National Marine Fisheries Service. The Northeast Regional Stranding Network has facilities at various spots along the Atlantic coast of the U.S. Participating researchers hold a federal permit authorizing them to direct rescue operations for strandings in their area. Their responsibilities include rehabilitating and releasing animals, when advisable, or placing those blinded or otherwise handicapped in suitable facilities.

While grants are awarded by the National Marine Fisheries Service (among others), a stranding center's lifeline is dependent on the donations and volunteers from the community. All of the centers have educational programs, as well as sponsored events such as whale watching excursions.

Humphrey, the lost humpback whale was perhaps the nation's most beloved and beleaguered media star throughout October of 1985. On a foggy Friday evening, the lone bull had cruised silently beneath the blinking lights of the Golden Gate Bridge into the San Francisco Bay, where his unusual odyssey captured the attention of the Coast Guard and the imagination of the international press. Humphrey, approximately forty-five feet (fourteen meters) long and weighing about forty tons (forty-four metric tons), had been migrating south—from Alaska to the humpback's breeding grounds in Hawaii—when he took a sudden detour, swimming instead more than seventy-five miles (forty-six kilometers) up the Sacramento River. While no one knows for certain what attracted Humphrey to this densely populated port, one theory is that he was drawn by an underwater signal resonating from one of the bay's military defense systems.

For twenty-five days, the California highways were jammed with whale-watchers who parked along the river banks to observe the scientists and volunteers as they tried to lead the animal out of one of the world's largest land-locked harbors. In the meantime, the National Fisheries Service moved to ensure crowd control by putting the disoriented marine mammal under federal protection—a legal precaution that carried a penalty of up to $20,000 for anyone convicted of "visible harassment" of the hapless humpback.

© Ken W. Davis/Tom Stack & Associates

CHAPTER EIGHT

Tributes to the Sea Monster

Killer whales are resented for their supposed interference with commercial fishing.

The whalers seem determined to honor their opponent in word and deed. This sentiment is evident in the crafting of scrimshaw (articles carved from whalebone) and the spinning of sea yarns. People of every nation had beliefs linking whales to the realm of the supernatural.

Especially frightening was the tale of the sea monster called Leviathan, a legend that prospered with the Mediterraneans. Combined of equal parts whale and serpent, he was described as four acres wide with a gravelly hide, festooned with tree-like growths and barnacles, much like a floating forest. When he slept on the ocean floor, sailors were cautioned not to set anchor in Leviathan's burled back; when he surfaced, they must not mistake him for an island. If aroused, Leviathan would sound like a breaching whale, and no sign would remain of the ship and its crew.

Whalers of all ethnic backgrounds respected the power of evil whales. To speak their name at sea was a dreaded taboo. The sound of an evil whale's name was thought to invoke a challenge that he would not ignore. It called him out from hidden depths to condemn the whaler who disturbed his peace. To avoid certain carnage, sailors would refer to the whale as a "great fish," a euphemism for the deadly whale.

Icelandic sailors believed that the whale delighted in a meal of human flesh. Any spot where a ship had gone down (or a man had drowned without the body being recovered) would be avoided for a full year. They were certain the whale, a clever beast, would remain in those waters until he got a second helping. For the same reason, villagers were leery of the docks where a whale had destroyed a ship, believing he might lunge from the deep to grab another human morsel off the shore.

On the other hand, the Vietnamese were convinced that whales were noble beasts sent by the god of the waters to protect fishermen. Rather than destroying boats, they believed the whales would aid sinking ships by allowing them to ride across their sturdy backs. The death of stranded whales was mourned by everyone in a Vietnamese village, with the most prominent citizen of the discovery party acting out the role of bereaved child. To the Vietnamese, the death of a whale meant the sky would pour with the tears of the water god in a raging storm that would last for three days. Villagers felt they had to locate the whale's corpse and give it a proper burial to calm the seas, which raged at the death of the whale.

© William B. Froelich/Envision

Mystic Seaport, Connecticut, houses one of the finest shipping museums in the United States. The whaling ship *Charles W. Morgan* is docked there permanently as a reminder of the nineteenth-century whaling industry.

New England whalers, staunch in their Christianity, had more practical concerns. When their boat was locked in combat with a particularly feisty whale, they would shout to one another, "Better have paid your washwoman!" The superstitution was that reneging on your washwoman's stipend while off at sea would result in the penalty of devastated deckboards.

At night, the whalers entertained each other with the exploits of man versus a monstrous old sperm whale called Caldera Dick. Many stories abound of the whaler who lost the battle only to win the war against the same whale much later on. A favorite is of the captain who lost his "iron," or anchor, to an escaping whale; thirteen years later while cutting up his haul, the captain found his iron, bearing his initials, in the great beast's blubber. Variations of the struggle of one man against one whale are found on every shore.

To pass the time, whalers embarked on a new folk art form—the scrimshonts or scrimshawing. A variety of small cutting tools were fashioned for shaping the teeth and jaw bone of the sperm whale into decorative items.

One of the small whaling boats stored on the *Charles W. Morgan* (left) seems no match for a wounded whale. In fact, whales were known to attack these small boats (above left), putting whalemen at peril in the rough seas.

Although elephant ivory is more valuable, sperm whale teeth were prized for centuries by scrimshaw artists. During idle periods at sea, whalers adorned whale bone and teeth with decorative carvings, usually with nautical themes.

The motifs were almost always nautical, often made in homage to a man's ship. Sometimes they were a finely detailed whaling scene. While the earliest carvings were on bone, more useful devices would follow. Scrimshaw flourishes were applied to trinket boxes, rolling pins, pie crimpers, and doorknobs. Scrimshaw busks and ornamental hairpins were labors of love, a symbol of a whaler's devotion to the woman he left behind. The busk was a narrow, flattened rod more elaborately decorated than other scrimshonds. Sentimental themes were often personalized by dates or initials. It was used as a mainstay in the front of ladies' corsets; inserted in a slit between the cleavage, it would hold up the bodice line. The gift was often accompanied by an original verse, imploring its recipient to always keep the absent whaler close to her heart.

Whalemen also conversed in their own language, creating a colorful new slang that would link all whalers from ship to ship and adventure to adventure. The whale and the industry that surrounded him was particularly well incorporated into New England phraseology. A harpooned whale will usually dive instantly and remain below for as long as an hour. When he surfaces again, it will be to "run," swimming at his highest speed and tugging at the harpoon line, skipping the boat like a pebble across the breaking water, taking the crew on a "Nantucket sleigh ride" which, to the wizened whaler, means an exciting rush.

"Skyscraper" was a word used long before the days of advanced architecture, meaning a tall ship whose mast could touch the clouds. On the shores of Maine, there were lookouts who sent up the cry of "towner!" It is an Indian word that means the whale has approached the coastline twice. To wish a sailor "greasy luck" was to hope he brought in a large haul of oil from the sperm whale. An ill shipmate might confide he was "pretty nigh fin out," an allusion to the dying whale, who rolls on his side in the water, showing one fin above the surface. Perhaps the most tested of these is "it takes a voyage to learn," a simple acknowledgment of experience's teacher. And, of course, today people are still having a "whale of a time."

CHAPTER NINE

A History of Greed and Shame

Nineteenth-century whaling has been romanticized in books, movies, and paintings, but hardships were many for sailors. This 1871 sketch by Benjamin Russell (right) shows the loss of thirty-three whaling ships in the Arctic, which were crushed or trapped by ice. An abandoned whaling station (far right) on Deception Island in Antarctica casts a ghostly vision of polar whaling practices.

North Wind Picture Archives

In some ways, the heroic romanticism surrounding the whalers was nothing more than clever packaging. Putting aside the tall tales, a whaler's life held no comfort and little reward. Most sailed on annual voyages. For the crew, each hunt was a crap shoot. Although a whaler's wages accumulated while isolated at sea, if the hunt was unsuccessful a man might well return indebted to his ship. However, if the haul was a grand one, a whaler could return rich beyond all reasonable expectations. It undoubtedly seemed a worthwhile gamble.

The hardships were many, chief among them the lack of fresh food, the damp clothing and bedding, and the grueling strain the work entailed. It was hardly a healthy life-style. Few of the men could stand upright below deck, the ceiling of which usually cleared only five feet. Provisions were restocked at infrequent ports and the ship was not supplied for emergencies; there was barely enough to last a single voyage. An Arctic whaler, forced by circumstances to winter aboard the vessel, was victimized by the ravages of

© Tim Gibson/Envision

starvation. As his health deteriorated, scurvy often followed. With the wracking body aches, the disease brought on severe depression and lethargy. All of this could have been cured by a well-planned food supply, rich in vitamin C; a head of cabbage or a few oranges could have brought life to a dying man. But there were none to be had.

Occasionally, if the hunt was slow, passing whaling ships would anchor off to visit one another. Aboard ship, a "gam," as it was called, would be the social event of the season.

In warmer regions, the whalers wrestled with their own demons. During the winter, when they docked, their contact with the natives was a woefully corrupting force. The whalemen brought the islanders European diseases and a taste for liquor. In New Zealand, they trafficked in shrunken heads. American whalers often picked up additional crew members from the islands. They were rarely paid and often abused, but they succeeded in their goal: entrance to the United States.

Modern whaling practices, despite the advantages of technology, are not substantially different from whale processing of old. Here, a baleen whale is hauled from the water to be processed.

© Bailey/Greenpeace

By 1909, motorboats from shore had joined the chase. The whaling era of the wooden sailing ships had ended by 1925. While the Americans and the Europeans had cast aside the old ways, many of the island crew members who had returned home continued to hunt in the old tradition. The practice was observed in the Solomon Islands, as well as in the Azores.

Although the sperm whale had been the favorite of early whalers, modern steam boats sparked interest in the faster-moving species towards the end of the nineteenth century. The North Atlantic became the prime hunting ground for blue whales, and, to a somewhat lesser degree, finbacks and sei whales. Shore whaling had widened the industry in the Antarctic as early as 1904. By the 1930s, oil manufacturing had reached a world-record high, with the regional output of Antarctic whale oil measuring 601,391 tons (approximately 540,000 metric tons). That sort of production required that 40,201 whales were killed, more than 73 percent of them were blue whales. As the decade drew to a close, it was obvious that the strain of the kill could not allow their numbers to replenish.

As a result, after World War II, the International Whaling Commission was formed. The commission first mandated that the catch be limited to baleens, of which the blue whale is the largest species. By the mid-1960s, blue whales in the southern hemisphere numbered less than 1,000. Fortunately, in 1963, the commission agreed on an overall protection for humpbacks, and finally extended their hunting ban to the blue whales. Yet, time and again, whalers simply turned their collective interests to other species —next to the finback. Finally, in 1966, the commission established an Antarctic catch limit covering all marine mammals. It was determined that the base figure should be less than the combined sustainable yield of the fin and sei whale stocks.

The International Whaling Commission was first formed in 1946 and has met every year since 1949. Its purpose is to set regulations appropriate to each country and species. In order to proceed, the commission is advised by a team of environmental scientists and biologists who research whale stock through statistics on breed capacity, age structure, and social/migratory dynamics. However, the commission must maintain a balance between what's good for the whales and what's good for the whalers. The whaling industry is based on a sizable capital and labor force. As a result,

Whales often are processed at sea on factory ships like this Soviet vessel (center) which leaves the seas bloody with discarded whale remains. Whales are defenseless against whaling ships (above right) that search for herds, harpoon them, and then are able to drag several at a time alongside the ship. A dead whale is hauled aboard a whaling ship (below right).

the economic complications of the commission's decisions are staggering.

Today, whaling is still an important industry and processing of the whales is done on large factory ships with several catcher boats. During the peak of the whaling era, a whale carcass was processed at a store station. This station was usually a compound of several buildings surrounding an immense slipway or "plan" on which the whales were placed. At the head of the plan were the winches used to hoist the animal from the water. At one side were the pressure boilers for meat and bone; on the other, the open boilers for blubber. Further on was the drying plant where the meat and bone was powdered after the oil was extracted. The rest of the compound was made up of machinery shops, a coal dump, oil tanks, worker's quarters, and, at its most remote end, the station manager's home. Shops may have sprung up to accommodate the workers' families, along with a chemist's lab for testing and controlling the manufacturing processes.

The whale's blubber is removed in long strips by a combination of the winches and the knives of the flensers. It is then taken aside and cut into smaller segments which are thrown down a chute into the revolving blades of a hack-knife. This minced meat is then cast into open boilers, where it is boiled until the oil runs off into the tanks. The rest of the carcass is stripped to the bone and processed in pressure boilers.

People have tried to make money using almost every part of the whale. But of its extensive product line, whale meat and meat extracts have proven the most profitable to the European whaler. In Japan, whale meat is highly regarded and more valuable than the whale's oil. Previous commercial ventures have also centered on the preparation of the whale's liver oil, which is high in vitamin A content. But the low cost of synthetic vitamin substances has left this practice unworthwhile. Other medical markets have briefly surfaced due to the enormous size of the whale's glandular structure, but the presumed demand for these natural hormones never surfaced. Likewise, the extraction of insulin from the whales' pancreas was not a commercial success. The least valuable commodity is bone dust. So after it is boiled for oil, any remaining fragments are discarded.

CHAPTER TEN

Last Call to Humanity

While whaling practices have been regulated since the formation of the International Whaling Commission (IWC) in 1946, conservationists and cetacean lovers argue that the IWC does not have enough power to regulate pirate whalers.

While the oceans may still seem lush with a multitude of fish and plant life, few species of marine mammals or reptiles remain. In fact, fourteen different types of whales have already been brought to the brink of extinction. Natural extinction leads to the development of a replacement species. When humans interfere with the ecological balance, however, no new animal evolves to take its place. Humans too often have depleted the natural riches of earth out of sheer ignorance.

While the whaling industry may be the most widespread threat to the survival of the cetacea, there are other more insidious threats to their survival. Ships have been known to kill whales by running them down. Hook and line fisheries have the lowest number of incidental kills, while fishery operations that use nets rack up a higher number of casualties. Towed gear, such as trawls, also accidentally catch unwary whales and other sea mammals. However, fixed nets most likely take the highest toll on the cetacean population, particularly during runs of fish. While smaller species of whale are often involved, incidental kills of this kind have the most profound effect on the dolphin population.

Incidental kills are also the result of increasing amounts of indestructible man-made refuse in our oceans. According to a 1985 report, merchant ships dump 450,000 plastic containers into international waters every day. Since the late 1970s, scientists have been documenting the far-reaching effects this plastic peril holds for all forms of marine life. By their estimates, plastic remnants annually account for the maiming or deaths of tens of thousands of seabirds, seals, sea lions, and sea otters as well as hundreds of whales, dolphins, porpoises, and sea turtles. And unlike oil or toxic chemical spills that limit their lethal potential to a controlled territory, plastics, according to David List of the U.S. Marine Commission, are "like individual mines floating around the ocean just waiting for victims." Whales who swallow plastic suffer from punctured stomach or intestinal linings, or may succumb to a strangulated respiratory system. A slower death awaits those whales who inadvertently entwine themselves in discarded plastic netting. The heads or tails of lunge-feeding whales often become so tightly wrapped that they are unable to eat or move properly. They usually starve or die of exhaustion.

The whaling industry has also made a considerable contribution to the decline in the whale population. Historically, whales have been considered an exploitable natural resource, which has decreased many of their number to dangerous levels. But the economics of the whaling industry have made regulating its activities to protect the cetacean population difficult.

Modern efforts to regulate whaling began in 1946 with the creation of the International Whaling Commission (IWC). While the United States took the lead in organizing the IWC, its concern was far from altruistic. Whaling offered a "free" and immediate resource that could provide valuable consumer goods like oil and meat, as well as profitable capital return to trading countries ravaged by World War II. A symbiotic relationship between the United States and Japan developed: The U.S. financed the Japanese whaling expeditions, receiving in return highly prized whale oil, while the Japanese kept the meat for domestic consumption. While the U.S. was not a major power in the whaling industry, it could still wield considerable power through its involvement in an international trade group.

Along with other nations, the U.S. insisted that, in order to uphold national sovereignty, all members of the IWC must be empowered to reject or uphold IWC recommendations at their own choosing. Ultimately, the jurisdiction of the IWC extended only to those nations that accepted it, of which there have been only between fifteen and twenty-three in the history of the Commission. In addition, any amendments to the IWC's regulations would require a three-fourths majority vote. But each nation could avoid being bound by these decisions simply by filing an objection within ninety days of their proclamation. Without a means for legal enforcement and with its scientific community bound by the power of a three-fourths vote, the IWC was an impotent savior. The fate of the whales would be determined by bargains made between large economic and political powers.

For example, when the IWC established a time limit on the hunting season in 1946, it succeeded in encouraging each nation to develop the most efficient vessels and killing techniques possible to maximize their share of the Antarctic quota. Each nation vigorously competed to outdo the others. Whalers wryly named it "the Whaling Olympics."

Today, regulations issued by the IWC are more specific and include guidelines on protected species, restricted hunting waters, catch limits and individual size requirements, the importing of whale-meat products, and special considerations on the taking of undersized whales for local consumption. Still, professional observers maintain that, based on historical precedence, the international whaling industry has never willingly agreed to regulate itself, or to restrict catch levels so that whaling could continue on an ecologically sound basis. In fact, efforts to side-step international regulatory measures have resulted in the development of what the IWC terms "outlaw" or "pirate" whaling. These unregulated operations are particularly threatening to the whales, as they do not follow even the most basic guidelines designed to promote the species survival.

Outlaw whaling operations persist for one reason only—they are highly profitable. The largest of these operations simply take the best cuts of meat and dump the remaining carcass back into the sea. When an outlaw factory catcher returns to port with its freezer filled with whale meat, it has probably killed twice as many whales as a ship operating under regulations.

Thanks to the concerted efforts of conservationists and government agencies, the United States has been responsible for focusing world-wide attention on many violators of the international moratorium on commercial whaling. Offending nations have included Japan and the Soviet Union (1974 and 1975); Chile, Peru, and South Korea (1978); and Norway (1986). For the most part, foreign governments have responded favorably to the threat of a U.S. trade embargo, although no sanctions have ever been imposed. Sadly, many whalers discontinue operations only while public attention is focused on their actions and soon return to their outlaw whaling once the furor has died down. Such circumstances often bring frustrated, extremist factions of the anti-whaling movement to violent gestures.

Conservationist ships have rammed and sunk outlaw whaling vessels. It's no surprise that the outlaw whalers learned to fight back. Spain's *Isba Three*, sister ship of two sunken catcher boats, posted armed guards in port and had a military escort accompany her to the whaling grounds. Outlaw whal-

Greenpeace (right), an international organization devoted to saving the whales, uses its fleet of boats to follow whaling practices and document outlaw whalers in action.

Below: Conservationists would argue that there are substitutes for whale meat, but not for whales.

ers have also developed a certain skill in the art of disguise. In the last ten years, they have perfected falsified product labels that make pirate meat appear to be the product of a legal operation. Special "dummy" companies have even been set up to "launder" whale meat of questionable origin.

Conservationists have suggested that until outlaw whaling can be brought to a complete halt, allowances for the pirate kill must be made when the IWC assigns its species quotas. An estimated "take" for the outlaw operation would be deducted from the regulated quotas of a particular hunting ground. This would protect the whales from double exploitation, while offering authorized whalers a valuable incentive for assisting the IWC in shutting down the outlaw whalers.

A poorly regulated whaling industry and the onset of high-tech refuse make maintaining accurate numbers on the surviving whales essential. Whales are extremely difficult, rare, and expensive subjects to study. One of the least disruptive methods is marking. Whales are "tattooed" with stainless steel darts, each bearing their own serial number, that are fired from a shotgun. Whalers who spot the marking while carving up their catch may claim a reward by cutting out the marked chunk of flesh. Such returns keep scientists abreast of migratory patterns within herds, but may also help to note changes in different breeding populations or determine a species' mortality rate.

Internationally, the whale has entered a new renaissance. Through the work of conservation groups and government regulatory agencies, people all over the world have been sensitized to the plight of marine mammals. Even in Japan, where their meat is a prized delicacy, whales and porpoises are the star attractions at aquariums and water shows. Nonetheless, we must become more keenly aware of each species' dependency on its habitat and on other organisms. By recognizing that there is a chain of life that connects all living things, we can help maintain that delicate balance to create an environment that helps them thrive.

Glossary

AFT At, near, or toward the stern of a ship.

AMBERGRIS A waxy, grayish substance found in the intestines of sperm whales; sometimes used in perfume.

AORTA The main artery of the body which carries blood from the left ventricle of the heart to all other parts of the body.

ARCHAEOCETE The name for ancient whales, now extinct, from which present-day cetacean life-forms developed.

BALEEN The fibrous plates attached to the upper jaw of whales of the mysticeti suborder, enabling them to filter krill and plankton from the water for food.

BARNACLE Any of a number of saltwater shellfish that attach themselves to rocks, wharves, ship bottoms, and whales.

BLOWHOLE Situated on the top of whales' heads, whales breathe through their blowholes.

BULWARK The extension of a ship's side above the deck.

BUSK A strip of whale bone that was used to stiffen the front of corsets.

CARNIVORE Referring to any mammals that eat only meat.

CAVUM VENTRALE The pouch in a whale's belly that expands to hold food and water.

CEREBELLUM The section of the brain consisting of two lateral lobes and a middle lobe that functions as the coordinating center for all muscular movement.

CEREBRAL CORTEX A part of the brain that refers to the outer part of external layers or the cerebrum.

CERVICAL Pertaining to the neck.

CETACEA An order of marine mammals that includes whales, dolphins, and porpoises.

CLASSIFICATION A class or group belonging to the system of taxonomy.

COPEPOD A small, sometimes parasitic crustacean that can live in either fresh or salt water.

CRUSTACEAN Members of the arthropod phylum including shrimps, crabs, barnacles, and lobsters; they usually live in the water, breathe through gills, and have a hard outer shell with jointed appendages.

DORSAL Designating the back of an animal.

ECHOLOCATION An acoustical system in which an animal navigates by means of reflected biomagnetic sound waves.

FISSURE A groove between lobes or parts of an organ, as in the brain.

FLANK The fleshy part of an animal found between the ribs and the hip or pelvic bones.

FLENSE The process of cutting blubber or skin from a whale or seal.

FLIPPERS The pectoral paddles, or forelimbs, of a marine mammal.

FLUKES The two horizontal lobes of a cetacean's tail fin.

FOLLICLE Any small cavity or gland which secretes or excretes; for example, the pore that holds a single hair.

GENUS A classification of plants or animals that share common distinguishing characteristics; genus is the main subdivision of a family and it is further divided into species.

GUSTATORY Referring to the sense of taste.

HERBIVOROUS Any species that feeds chiefly on plant life.

INCIDENTAL KILL The death of an animal not caused by hunting, but occurring as the secondary result of some other organized effort, usually involving an industrial operation.

ISOPODS An order of mostly aquatic crustaceans, isopods have flat, oval bodies with seven pairs of fully functional legs attached to individual segments of the thorax.

KRILL Small, shrimp-like crustaceans that form the mainstay of the baleen whale's diet.

LICE The plural of louse, they are small wingless insects (from the Anoplura order) characterized by sucking oral cavities that enable them to live as parasites on other mammals.

MAMMAL A warm-blooded, vertebrate animal that suckles its young through mammary secretions.

MELON The bulbous forehead of certain odontoceti (toothed) whales which often contains oil.

MYOGLOBIN An iron-based protein, similar to hemoglobin, that is found in muscle tissue that holds large amounts of oxygen.

MYSIDS Small crustacean with two branch-like appendages and a horny, protective shell covering most of its thorax.

MYSTICETI A suborder of the cetacea comprised of the baleen or whalebone whales.

NEOTENY In zoology, the retention of juvenile characteristics in the adult of a species, or the development of adult features in the juvenile (such as the attainment of sexual maturity in some larvae).

ODONTOCETI The suborder of the cetacea comprised of toothed whales.

ORDER A group of related organisms that ranks between a family and a class.

PALEONTOLOGY The branch of geology that deals with prehistoric life forms; a paleontologist studies plant and animal fossils to construct his theories on the earth's past.

PARASITES Plants or animals that live on or in another organism from which they derive sustenance or shelter without benefiting the host organism, often harming it over a period of time.

PIZZLE The penis of an animal or a whip made from the penis of a bull or whale.

PLANKTON Mostly microscopic plant or animal life found passively drifting in the upper layers of the ocean.

POLYCHAETES A classification of marine annelid worms, characterized by fleshy, bristle-covered, segmented appendages.

PRIMATE Mammals of the Primata order which includes lemurs, monkeys, apes, and man. They are particularly distinguished by their flexible hands and feet, all of which have five digits.

PROW The forward part of a boat or ship, also called the bow.

RAIL A narrow wooden piece at the top of a ship's bulwark.

RAMIFIED Spread out into branch-like divisions.

RORQUAL Any baleen whale with numerous longitudinal pleats or grooves on its throat and belly.

ROSTRUM A beak-like projection that, in the cetacean, is usually an extension of the upper jaw.

SCRIMSHAW At one time the exclusive work of sailors, it is the decorative art of carving on shells, bone, and ivory.

SCURVY A disease attributed to a lack of Vitamin C and distinguished by anemia, fatigue, spongy gums, and bleeding from the mucous membranes.

SHREW Any of the small, mouse-like species belonging to the Sorcidae family of mammals.

SOUND When pertaining to whales or large fish, it is the sudden act of diving deeply.

SPECIES The fundamental category of a taxonomic classification, comprising a subdivision of a genus and defining a group of interbreeding animals.

SPERMACETI A white, waxy substance taken from the pool of oil in the head of a sperm whale or dolphin. It is often used to manufacture cosmetics, ointments, and candles.

STERN The rear end of a ship or boat.

STRANDING The state of a marine mammal aground and unable to alter its situation or deal with its present environment, as when a whale is beached.

SUBSPECIES Any subdivision of a species that exhibits small but persistent variations from others of the same species; often a geographically altered distinction.

TACTILE Referring to the sense of touch.

TAXONOMY A system of identifying animals and plants by arranging them in groups based on common characteristics.

TERRESTRIAL A creature or organism that lives on the land rather than in the water, air, or trees.

THORAX In man and other higher vertebrates, the part of the body between the neck and abdomen. In insects or crustaceans, thorax refers to the middle of three main segments.

TRAWL A large, baglike net dragged by a boat along the bottom of a fishing bank.

TUBERCLE A small, rounded knoblike elevation of the skin or hide.

VENTRAL Referring to the belly or abdomen of an animal.

VERTEBRATE An animal with a backbone, a segmented spinal column, and an enclosed brain.

VESTIGIAL Referring to a rudimentary part or organ, now characterized as degenerate or atrophied, that was probably more fully functional in an earlier stage of species development.

WHALEBONE See "Baleen."

WINCH A cranklike apparatus for hoisting or hauling, operated by hand or machine, and consisting of a drum or cylinder upon which a rope or cable is wound that is also attached to the object to be lifted or hauled; the act of hoisting or hauling with the use of a winch.

Bibliography

Attenborough, David, *Life On Earth*, (Boston and Toronto: Little, Brown and Company, 1979).

Beck, Horace, *Folklore and the Sea*, (Middletown, Connecticut: Wesleyan University Press, 1973).

Botkin, B. A., *A Treasurey of New England Folklore*, (New York: Crown Publishers, 1965).

Burton, Maurice, *Systematic Dictionary of Mammals of the World*, (New York: Thomas Y. Crowell, 1962).

Burton, Richard, *The Life and Death of Whales*, (New York: Universe Books, 1973).

Caras, Roger A., *Last Chance on Earth*, (New York and Philadelphia: Chilton Books, 1966).

Cousteau, Jacques-Yves with James Dugan, *The Living Sea*, (New York and Evanston: Harper & Row, 1963).

Cousteau, Jacques-Yves with Philippe Diole, translation by J. F. Bernard, *The Whale: Mighty Monarch of the Sea*, (New York: Doubleday, 1972).

Curry-Lindahl, Kai, *Let Them Live: A Worldwide Survey of Animals Threatened with Extinction*, (New York: William Morrow & Company, 1972).

Fichtelius, Karl-Erik and Sverre Sjolander, *Smarter Than Man? Intelligence in Whales, Dolphins and Humans*, (New York: Pantheon Books, 1972).

Flayderman, E. Norman, *Scrimshaw and Scrimshanders: Whale and Whalemen*, (New Milford, Connecticut: N. Flayderman & Co., 1972).

Gilmore, Michael T., *Twentieth Century Interpretations of Moby-Dick*, (Englewood Cliffs, New Jersey: Prentice-Hall, 1977).

Gaunt, William, *Marine Painting: A Historical Survey,* (New York: Viking Press, 1975).

Harrison, G. B., *The Bible for Students of Literature and Art*, (New York: Doubleday and Company, 1964).

Hoyt, Erich, *The Whale Watcher's Handbook,* (New York: Madison Press Books/Doubleday & Company, 1984).

Lockley, Ronald M., *Whales, Dolphins, and Porpoises,* (New York: W. W. Norton & Co., 1979).

Matthews, L. Harrison ed., *The Whale*, (New York: Simon and Schuster, 1968).

McNulty, Faith, *The Great Whales*, (New York: Doubleday, 1973).

National Geographic Society, *The Marvels of Animal Behavior*, (Natural Science Library/National Geographic Book Service, 1972).

Perry, Richard, *The Unknown Ocean*, (New York: Taplinger Publishing Company, 1972).

Robotti, Frances Diane, *Whaling and Old Salem*, (New York: Fountainhead Publishers, 1962).

Schmitt, Frederick P., *Mark Well the Whale!*, (Port Washington, New York: Ira J. Friedman Division/Kennikat Press, 1971).

Slijper, E. J., translated by A. J. Pomerans, *Whales*, (New York: Basic Books, 1962).

Small, George, *The Blue Whale*, (New York: Columbia University Press, 1972).

Stein, Roger B., *Seascape and the American Imagination*, (New York: Clarkson N. Potter, 1975).

Sweeney, James B., *A Pictorial History of Sea Monsters and Other Dangerous Marine Life,*, (New York: Bonanza Books, 1972).

Thorson, Gunnar, translation by Manon C. Meilgaard and Alec Laurie, *Life in the Sea*, (New York and Toronto: World University Library/McGraw-Hill, 1971).

Watson, Lyle. *Sea Guide to Whales of the World*, (New York: E. P. Dutton, 1981).

Wilmerding, John, *A History of American Marine Painting*, (Boston and Toronto: Little, Brown and Company, 1968).

Winn, Louis and Howard Winn, *Wings in the Sea*, (Boston: University Press of New England, 1985).

Articles

Bartlett, Kay. " 'Thar She Blows!' Cape Cod's Whale Trails," *The Record*, (Bergen County, New Jersey), October 18, 1987.

Bon, Amy. "Marine Biologists Get Rare Opportunity," *Sentinel*, (Santa Cruz, Calif.), May 7, 1986.

Clavin, Thomas. "Increase in Whales Puzzles Scientists," *New York Times*, (New York, N.Y.), August 16, 1987.

Meacham, Jody. "A Whale of an Illustrator," *Mercury News*, (San Jose, Calif.), April 9, 1987.

Miller, Donald. "Illustrating the Natural World," *Sentinel*, (Santa Cruz, Calif.), April 14, 1987.

Netter, Thomas W. "Conservationists Fear Breakdown in Whaling Moratorium," *New York Times*, (New York, N.Y.), August 9, 1986.

Journals, Reports, Transcripts & Member Publications

Barnes, Lawrence G. "Outline of Eastern North Pacific Fossil Cetacean Assemblages," Reprinted from *Systematic Zoology*, Volume 25, Number 4, December 1976.

Barnes, Lawrence G. "Search for the First Whale: Retracing the Ancestry of Cetaceans," *Oceans*, March–April 1984.

Barnes, Lawrence G. "Whales, Dolphins and Porpoises: Origin and Evolution of Cetacea," Reprinted from *Mammals: Notes on a Short Course*, (University of Tennessee, Department of Geological Studies), 1984.

Barnes, Lawrence G. and Edward Mitchell. "Cetacea," Reprinted from *Evolution of African Mammals*, (Cambridge: Harvard University Press), 1978.

Barnes, Lawrence G. and Rodney E. Raschke, Joan C. Brown. "A Fossil Baleen Whale from the Capistrano Formation in Laguna Hills, California," The Natural Sciences of Orange County, (Huntington Beach, Calif.: Natural History Foundation), January 1, 1984.

Carter, Nick and Alan Thorton. "Pirate Whaling 1985 and a History of the Subversion of International Whaling Regulations," Environmental Investigation Agency, (Glasgow, Scotland: Society Against Violation of the Environment, Intl.), 1985.

Davies, Gareth Huw. "Japanese Whaling in the Philippines," Greenpeace Environmental Trust, (London, England: Calvert's Press (TU), Workers' Cooperative), 1986.

Downs, Hugh. "Congratulations, It's a Whale," 20/20 transcripts, (New York: Journal Graphics), Show #733, August 27, 1987.

Greenpeace. "Outlaw Whalers," (Washington, D.C.: Greenpeace Environmental Trust), Report issues 1980, 1981, 1982.

Greenpeace. "Scientific Whalers? The History of Whaling Under Special Permits," (Washington, D.C.: Greenpeace Environmental Trust), 1985.

Greenpeace. "Unregulated Whaling," (Washington, D.C.: Greenpeace Environmental Trust), 1983.

Institute of Marine Sciences. "Listening to Marine Mammals," *Science News*, (University of California, Santa Cruz), Volume 1, Number 1, Spring 1983.

Institute of Marine Sciences. "Whales of the Central California Coast," *IMS News*, (University of California, Santa Cruz), Volume 10, Number 9, Winter 1987.

M'Gonigle, R. Michael. "The Economizing of Ecology: Why Big, Rare Whales Still Die," (University of California, Berkeley), 1980.

Plowden, Campbell and Yuri Kusuda. "Small-Type Commercial Whaling in Japan," (Washington, D.C.: The Humane Society of the United States), June 1987.

Videography

The Great Whales. (Stamford, Connecticut: Vestron Video/National Geographic Series, 1987).

Life on Earth. (Burbank, Calif.: Warner Home Video, 1987).

The Sea Around Us. (Los Angeles, Calif.: The Nostalgia Merchant/Media Home Entertainment, 1953).

The Warm-Blooded Sea: Mammals of the Deep. (Burbank, Calif.: The Cousteau Odyssey Video Treasures/Warner Home Video, 1986).

Organizations

The following institutions provided research assistance and referral services instrumental in the completion of this volume:

GREENPEACE
1611 Connecticut Avenue, N.W.
Washington, D.C. 20009

MARINE MAMMAL STRANDING CENTER
P.O. Box 773
Brigantine, New Jersey 08203

NATURAL HISTORY MUSEUM OF LOS ANGELES COUNTY
Earth Sciences Division
900 Exposition Boulevard
Los Angeles, California 90007

OKEANOS OCEAN RESEARCH FOUNDATION
216 E. Montauk Highway
P.O. Box 776
Hampton Bays, New York 11946

SCRIPPS INSTITUTION OF OCEANOGRAPHY
University of California at San Diego
A-033B
La Jolla, California 92093

UNIVERSITY OF CALIFORNIA AT SANTA CRUZ
Marine Sciences Division
and their public interest support group:
FRIENDS OF LONG MARINE LABORATORY
c/o Institute of Marine Sciences
UCSC
Santa Cruz, California 95064

THE WHALING MUSEUM
Box 25, Cold Spring Harbor
Long Island, New York 11724

Index